AMERI

CRI

IC
A
N
SIS

Photographs for MAGNUM edited by Charles Harbutt and Lee Jones

AMERICA IN CRISIS

Text by Mitchel Levitas

A Ridge Press Book Holt, Rinehart and Winston, New York

Members of MAGNUM:

Eve Arnold
Cornell Capa
Bruce Davidson
Elliott Erwitt
Burt Glinn
Philip Jones Griffiths
Charles Harbutt
Danny Lyon
Constantine Manos
Donald McCullin
Wayne Miller
Dennis Stock
Burk Uzzle

Contributors:

Hiroji Kubota
Roger Malloch
Mary Ellen Mark
Paul Ryan
Rick Winsor

Copyright 1969 in all countries of the International Copyright Union by The Ridge Press, Inc., Holt, Rinehart and Winston, Inc., and Magnum Photos. All rights reserved throughout the world. Reproduction forbidden without prior written permission of the Publisher. Prepared and produced by The Ridge Press. Published simultaneously in Canada by Holt, Rinehart and Winston of Canada, Limited. Printed in Italy by Mondadori, Verona. Library of Congress Catalog Card Number: 69-16186 (cloth) SBN 03-081020-5   (paper) SBN 03-081247-X

Editor-in-Chief: *Jerry Mason*
Editor: *Adolph Suehsdorf*
Art Director: *Albert Squillace*
Associate Editor: *Moira Duggan*
Associate Editor: *Barbara Hoffbeck*
Art Associate: *David Namias*
Art Associate: *Egbert Teague*
Art Production: *Doris Mullane*

Contents

Foreword

Our crisis today is the clash between the nation's traditional vision of itself—the American dream—and the hard, discordant realities it lives with.

The dream has always been the light on our horizon, receding as we advanced, beckoning us on, an expression of confidence in the inexhaustible possibilities of America. Usually it has contained elements reflecting an American consensus, but it has never been precise and never has had to be. In every era of our past it has been flexible and accommodating, with headroom for every man's aspirations.

Heretofore, whether or not it was in fact, the dream has seemed attainable. Our undeniable social and economic progress has seemed to be consonant with it and proof of its validity. If as individuals we traveled toward the horizon at different rates of speed, the road was open to all, and missteps and wrong turnings were certain to be repaired in time.

Today events mock the dream. Large segments of our population experience it as a cruel mirage. Some, angered, reject the dream as beyond attainment. Some, frustrated, see their path as cleverly obstructed. Some, disillusioned, deny the dream's existence.

Even those who believe in it find their faith under test. For in an unaccustomed way we are confronted by uncomfortable evidence of distorted values, of lapsed standards, of rents in the fabric of the dream. In a land of liberty, we kill good men among us. In a land of plenty, poverty is ingrained. Professing social justice, we endure a shameful gap between what we say and what we do. We have floundered in a war that upheld our honor and degraded our principles. We have split with many of our youth. Events overwhelm us; our systems, for all their power, seem inadequate to their tasks. And our national spirit seems to have lost a measure of its generosity and zest.

America In Crisis is an effort to examine the dream and the reality. In text and pictures it seeks to identify the events, the trends, and the feelings involved in this crucial period of the American experience. Because so much of what is happening is subjective, much of the crisis is interpreted in pictures. All photographs are the work of Magnum, the international cooperative of photojournalists. The text has been written by Mitchel Levitas, an editor of *The New York Times Magazine*, who has been a Nieman Fellow and a winner of the George Polk Award for outstanding metropolitan reporting.

Editorially, it has seemed reasonable to define the current condition of the United States as a crisis—not certainly the first in our history, but one we now must come to grips with. Taking its measure may be a step toward surmounting it and toward making all citizens eligible to share the dream.

The Editors

The American Dream

I have a dream today.

Martin Luther King, Jr.
March on Washington,
August 28, 1963

*You can see why I believe so deeply
in the American dream.*

Richard M. Nixon
accepting the Presidential
nomination in Miami,
August 8, 1968

Somewhere between the life and the dream, between the myths and the realities, lies the meaning of the American experience. Like all national histories, it has been shaped by accident as well as by design, by leaders who forged a popular mood as well as by those who followed one, by periods of tumultuous social change, and by years of stagnation. More than most countries, though, the United States has been guided by basic assumptions concerning its character as a nation and the personality of its people. Many of these convictions, reaching back to a time before nationhood, survive to the present. Like a hall of mirrors reflecting or distorting the truth, this set of beliefs is a corridor to the past in which the American dream was born.

First among the articles of faith was belief in America's uniqueness—unique in untapped riches, in its freedom-seeking settlers, in the three thousand miles of ocean that was a welcome barrier between the old civilization of Europe and the new continent. In the Colonies a man was separate from his ancestors; the bonds of class were severed; he could begin fresh, limited only by ambition and ability. Here would be built God's American Israel, Reinhold Niebuhr has said, whose children would be free. Except for the slaves, equality of opportunity was a fact, not a slogan, as the emerging nation itself bore witness.

"Here they are become men," wrote Hector St. Jean de Crèvecoeur in "Letters from an American Farmer," written during the Revolutionary era. "In Europe they were so many useless plants....They withered and were mowed down by want, hunger and war. *He* is an American who, leaving behind him all his ancient prejudices and manners, receives new ones from the new mode of life he has embraced and the new rank he holds....Here individuals of all nations are melted into a new race of men ...western pilgrims who are carrying along with them that great mass of arts, sciences, vigor and industry which began long since in the east. They will finish the circle." It was an optimistic, prophetic, and, for its time, a reasonably accurate appraisal.

Writing almost a century later, Baron von Hübner, an Austrian diplomat and traveler, attributed the growth and vigor of the quickly developing nation to "the magic charm of two words" which still embodied the American dream: liberty and equality. "The emigrants go to you," he said, "for bread, individual liberty and social equality, and they find space; that is, liberty to work and equality of success if they bring with them the necessary qualifications....In Europe a man works to live... here he works to become rich. Everyone does not attain this goal, but everyone tries for it."

Americans heard such words and believed them. Why not? The assumption that material progress was both good and natural seemed justified by the gold, timber, and grain that issued from the land. As one frontier was reached another beckoned, calling the young, the restless, and the hopeful farther and farther West. According to the nineteenth-century historian, Frederick Jackson Turner, it was the frontier that cradled and nourished American democracy. It confirmed optimism, made men equal, brought law and order. As the pioneers moved on, those who followed renewed the myths that shaped the nation's self-image: hard work and a belief in the future; universal education for universal opportunity; tranquil, neighborly, rural towns governed by participatory democracy; a spirit of tolerance that contrasted with Europe's strife and encouraged the notion that America was morally superior. Extending the Republic from coast to coast, uprooting foreign colonial outposts and slaughtering Indians, fulfilled what later would be called our Manifest Destiny.

Today our destiny no longer seems manifest. On the contrary, it seems to many uncertain. Undermining historic self-confidence, suspicion grows that luck is beginning to run out, that the bright side of the dream is being eclipsed by the dark side. It is a painful recognition, but not new. One of the most famous visitors to America, Charles Dickens, commented about Americans, "It would be well if they loved the real less and the ideal more." Writers and poets from Hawthorne to Ginsberg have pointed to the contradictions that held the dream in tension: affluence and waste, ambition and greed, peace and violence. The ambiguity was expressed by Robinson Jeffers:

You make haste on decay: not blameworthy;
      life is good,
  be it stubbornly long or suddenly
A mortal splendor: meteors are not needed less than
      mountains: shine, perishing republic.

Parts of the dream are undoubtedly perishing. In less than two generations a nation of farmers has become a nation of workers; in the last half-century the proportion of Americans living on working farms has dropped from about thirty-three per cent to about five-and-a-half per cent. The quiet and prosperous small town is a vanishing memory. "The only middle-class group whose children generally do not leave the small towns are the marginal retail merchants who often have little to bequeath except their business," two sociologists report. "The limits of recovery have been set by shopkeeper mentalities." As the migration to urban centers continues — more than eighteen million people in two decades, two million of them Negroes—the cities struggle to accommodate the waves of immigrants.

American inventiveness has produced the most advanced technology on earth, but the country seems to be producing more and enjoying it less. The worship of youth as instigators of innovation and reform has been transformed, in the words of one critic, into "war against the young." The myth of equality is confronted by the fact of racism. Affluence barely conceals our twenty-five million poor. Mobility creates rootlessness; pursuing internal frontiers, the average family stays in one place for no more than five years. The speed of social change is greater than our institutions can harness, causing communities and individuals to lose the sense that they can control their own future. A people which has enjoyed peace and stability for most of its history turns inward to find itself divided and angry.

21

Streak of Violence

At a time when a century is measured by a generation, and a generation by a decade, the six years since John F. Kennedy was assassinated in Dallas seem to have passed in a moment. The shot still echoes, a memory renewed by unthinkable repetition. Martin Luther King, Jr., who had rallied Negroes to action and touched the conscience of whites, was killed by a sniper in Memphis on April 4, 1968. Two months later Robert F. Kennedy was murdered in the passageway of a hotel kitchen in Los Angeles, minutes after narrowly winning a Democratic Presidential primary election. "What is this all about?" asked Richard Cardinal Cushing, who had mourned with the Kennedy family on other occasions. "We could continue our prayers that it would never happen again, but we did that before." Again, as before, the nation's shock and lamentation was punctuated by the Cardinal's question: "What is this all about?"

Did the series of assassinations mark a high point in a society's normal ebb and flow of violence that would, in time, recede? Did it only prove the existence of psychopaths in a population of two hundred million? Was the violence "structural"—the result of an intersecting and overlapping complex of institutional practices: the tradition of armed police; the prevalence of mayhem in the mass media; the refusal of Congress to pass tough gun-control legislation despite the menace of one hundred million privately owned handguns, shotguns, and rifles? Finally, was the society by nature violent? As James Reston wrote on the day that President Kennedy was killed: "America wept tonight, not alone for its dead young President, but for itself.... Somehow the worst in the nation had prevailed over the best...something in the nation itself, some strain of madness and violence had destroyed the highest symbol of law and order."

Most answers were inconclusive, and a few were contradictory. Some explained the assassinations as evidence that the democratic spirit was dead—that the United States was as "barbarically corrupt" at home as it was in Vietnam. Others saw them as inversions of the democratic spirit—as the perverse attempts of flawed individuals to redress the imbalance of a society where stress on achievement makes failure seem intolerable.

Amidst the drumbeat of debate rose words of reassurance. While it would be "self-deceptive to ignore the connection between lawlessness and hatred and this act of violence," President Johnson said after Robert Kennedy was shot, "it would be just as deceptive...to conclude from this act that the country is sick, that it has lost its balance, that it has lost its sense of direction, even its common decency. Two hundred million Americans did not strike down Robert Kennedy last night any more than they struck down John F. Kennedy in 1963 or Dr. Martin Luther King in April...."

The streak of individual violence runs deeper than most Americans admit. In 1967, guns were involved in 7,700 murders and 10,000 suicides. Although the number of southern lynchings has declined sharply in recent years, the U.S. Civil Rights Commission counted 2,595 lynchings in the South between 1882 and 1959. Whether the rising crime was statistical or real, the rising fear rate was indisputable. In part it was propelled by the outbursts of madmen. In July, 1966, Richard Speck methodically murdered eight student nurses in Chicago; the next month, Charles Whitman stabbed to death his wife and mother, then climbed to a tower on the campus of the University of Texas in Austin and in a spray of rifle fire killed thirteen more people; in November, Robert Smith, a Mesa, Arizona, youth, shot and killed four women and a child.

Collective violence in the United States, while usually provoked by "rational" motives, is equally ferocious. "We began, after all," the historian Arthur Schlesinger said, "as a people who killed red men and enslaved black men." Colonial history records a succession of riots by the desperate poor: Bacon's Rebellion, Shay's Rebellion, and the Whiskey Rebellion. The nineteenth century witnessed slave revolts, Civil War draft riots in which almost two thousand people died, riots against the Irish and Chinese, and the march on Washington of Coxey's Army of unemployed. The century closed with bloody struggles for union recognition by workers in Homestead, Pennsylvania, and Pullman, Illinois, a conflict that reached its climax in the industrial violence of the 1930's and only subsided when the Federal government intervened to give workers the right to bargain collectively, and strike if necessary, for better wages and working conditions.

Nor are racially inspired urban riots a historical novelty. Between 1917 and 1921, major riots by whites against Negroes broke out in nine cities, including Washington, D.C. The worst erupted in Chicago in 1919 when a Negro boy, swimming at a segregated beach, drifted into nearby waters reserved for whites and was drowned—perhaps hit by a stone, as Negroes charged. Police refused to arrest a white man and instead arrested a Negro. Fighting ensued and soon spread to the inner city. After nearly a week of sporadic warfare the toll included more than two dozen dead and several hundred injured and wounded by gunfire. During World War II a second wave of racial riots hit Harlem, Detroit, and several other big cities, although relatively few G.I.'s at the front heard the news. In 1943, in Harlem, mass violence was touched off when a white policeman tried to arrest a Negro woman who was defended by a Negro soldier. That same year in Detroit a much fiercer and costlier riot was preceded by months of growing racial strife. More than fifty thousand Negroes had recently arrived in the city, drawn by the promise of jobs in defense plants. The ghetto spilled into previously white neighborhoods, breeding anger and occasional fights. During the same period, wildcat strikes broke out among white factory workers to protest enforcement of Federal regulations requiring the fair treatment of Negro workers. Such reactions were perhaps instinctive on the part of many white southern workers who also had migrated to Detroit in search of better jobs. And in the event that their instincts required encouragement to action, a formidable trio of incendiary white supremacists — Gerald L.K. Smith, Frank J. Norris, and Father Charles Coughlin—was at hand to goad them. At least the current wave of urban rioting is notable for the absence of white agitators, but that is small comfort compared to the desperation which leads Negroes to set the torch to their homes.

Collective violence is a somber part of the American tradition, often forcing social reform when political leadership fails. Negro sociologist Kenneth Clark, no advocate of riots, calls violence "the cutting edge of justice." The assassination of three national figures within five years was thus particularly tragic. If John and Robert Kennedy and Martin Luther King, Jr., promised anything, they promised the hope of peaceful change. Among the poor, the young, and the black, the common reaction was, "*They* killed him." With the murder of King, the spokesman for nonviolence, a spasm of rage and grief seized Negroes in more than one hundred and thirty cities. A people's most powerful voice had been silenced just when it was most needed, to lead another march on Washington for all the poor of the nation.

Mrs. Martin Luther King, Jr.

Mrs. John F. Kennedy

Mrs. Robert F. Kennedy

Memphis: Plane bearing body of Martin Luther King takes off for Atlanta.

Washington, D.C.: Boots reversed in stirrups were symbol of President Kennedy's death.

En route: Robert Kennedy is borne to Washington.

New York City

New Jersey

Memphis, Tennessee

The Deep Roots of Poverty

Poverty isn't what it used to be. Franklin Roosevelt's "one-third of a nation" has shrunk to between fifteen and twenty per cent. The temporary props of the New Deal—the WPA, NRA, CCC—have given way to a carefully planned long-range "war on poverty." Confidence in the capitalist system, shared by all but the most romantic radicals, has replaced depression panic that the system was doomed. Not even staunch Marxists believe the United States is in a "pre-revolutionary" phase, let alone ripe for revolution.

But if poverty is now less extensive, it is more stubbornly resistant to attack. If the professed national goal is the eradication—not merely the amelioration—of poverty, the target is more distant than ever. And if the fabulously successful economic system, which has more than doubled the gross national product in a decade, awards $20,000 annual incomes to the nation's top twelve million families, it still provides only a bare subsistence income of $2,000 a year to the bottom twelve million families. Will Rogers joked that America was "the only nation in the history of the world that went to the poorhouse in an automobile." Nowadays, television antennas project from the roofs of rural shanties and slum tenements. But as the upper and middle classes have grown richer, the poor have stayed put. The contrast between affluence and poverty has sharpened, and it is commonplace to observe that television has done much to awaken the poor to a recognition of the contrast.

But if the poor are more aware, so are the privileged — a belated acknowledgement of inequality that goes far toward explaining the profound dissatisfactions gnawing at the American conscience. How much longer can the richest nation on the planet and the wealthiest in man's history tolerate the hunger, sickness, and despair of millions of its citizens? How much longer can Americans hear praise for their moral fiber, while the fiber is corroded by guilt and envy? How much longer will they plow under crops and bulldoze new highways for suburbanites, while children grow up mentally retarded for lack of nourishment and families are made homeless for the sake of saving twenty-two minutes of driving time? Such questions were irrelevant in the Thirties. Not now, when considerations of poverty and prosperity have become inseparable.

Contemporary poverty differs in two other respects from the poverty of the Thirties. The burdens of the Great Depression fell impartially upon white and black. Today, two out of every three people below the official poverty line are white. But the burden of poverty falls disproportionately on the Negro. About twelve per cent of the white population is impoverished as compared to forty-one per cent of Negroes. Moreover, an alarming thirty-five per cent of the urban poor are black, thereby intensifying political tensions in the cities and complicating the strategy of the "war" against poverty. Second, the attitude of the poor toward their own poverty has changed considerably. As Robert Bendiner has pointed out, "The difference, quite simply, is the difference between a feeling of temporary exclusion from the good things of one's society and deprivation as a permanent, even hereditary, way of life. To be sure, many of the temporarily dispossessed in the days of the Depression did give way to despair...and their lot was tragic. But there were more who were certain that with the recovery of the economy their fortune would rise again....In short, there was hope and spirit, or at the very least, the feeling of being in the same boat as half the population of the country."

Isolated from an affluent society, the contemporary poor are denied even the satisfaction that accompanies a sense of belonging. Unlike the penniless immigrants of an earlier era who accepted initial deprivation in exchange for the hope the country promised, most of today's poor are at a dead end. Defining what is technically known as the "cycle of poverty," a report by a United States Senate Committee declared: "Poverty in America tends to be a permanent state, concentrated among certain disadvantaged groups and in many cases continuing generation after generation." Such poverty persists despite record prosperity, widening job opportunities, and a proliferation of social services such as health care, welfare allotments, subsidized housing, and cheap food.

The workers and middle-class professionals of the Thirties were skilled, educated, and potentially employable; today's poor are largely unskilled and unemployable. They are also "increasingly invisible," as Michael Harrington wrote in *The Other America* — one of those rare books which helped move an entire government to action. "Many of the poor," Harrington said, "are the wrong age to be seen." According to one study which numbered the nation's poor at thirty-five million, fifteen million are under eighteen, and five million are over sixty-five. About thirty per cent of all citizens over sixty-five live in poverty; about twenty-five per cent of all children under eighteen are poor. For the elderly, it is too late to find work. For the young, it is extremely difficult. Reared among families who are themselves usually poorly educated and apathetic, children of poverty start life enormously handicapped. More than a third leave school by the eighth grade. Without skills and without much chance of acquiring them, their feelings of resentment, rejection, and defeat begin early and grow rapidly. "Born losers" is more than a phrase.

A poor American is four times as likely to die before the age of thirty-five as is the average citizen. Infant mortality is twice as high among the poor, one reason why the United States ranks eighteenth among nations in the rate of infant deaths. Almost sixty per cent of the poor suffer from more than one disabling physical condition, compared to twenty-four per cent among the better-off. Even medical research seems to favor the upper classes. Medicine's major triumphs have been over acute, not chronic, disorders.

According to "Hunger, U.S.A.," a report by the Citizen's Board of Inquiry into Hunger and Malnutrition in the U.S., some ten million Americans are chronically malnourished and some two hundred and eighty of the country's 3,100 counties are critical hunger areas. In one such Mississippi county, an antipoverty worker described a typical daily diet: "Breakfast will be grits, molasses and biscuit. For lunch the adults will eat nothing and the children who are at home will be given a piece of bread and a drink of Kool-Aid or water. The evening meal usually consists of boiled beans and corn bread." In particularly poor homes, "there is usually no table...and what little food there is is eaten by hand out of a bowl or from a newspaper on the floor." The insidious effects of poor nutrition — retarded growth, organic brain damage, higher vulnerability to disease—are well documented. So is the fact, reported in a U.S. Public Health Service investigation, that the "alarming" extent of malnutrition among a random sample of twelve thousand poor Americans was on a par with the results of surveys in South America.

Not only are the poor more liable to physical disorders, they also suffer psychological disabilities more frequently. Treated psychiatric illness was three times more prevalent among the poor than among the wealthy or middle classes, a study conducted in New Haven in the 1950's concluded. Also, among those treated, psychosis rather than neurosis was the characteristic form of emotional disease for ninety per cent of those in the lowest fifth on the economic scale. Only thirty-five per cent of the top four income groups were diagnosed as having psychotic disturbances. Not surprising is the following personality profile of the poor drawn by a Cornell University team in the 1950's but still valid: "[They are] rigid, suspicious and have a fatalistic outlook on life. They do not plan ahead. ...They are prone to depression, have feelings of futility, lack of belongingness, friendliness and a lack of trust in others."

About half the poor in the country are concentrated in the rural South and in Appalachia—the latter a territory of 185,000 square miles that stretches through thirteen states from the southern corner of New York to northern Mississippi. Many of Appalachia's seventeen million people — ninety-three per cent white—dwell in almost inaccessible mountain hollows, scratching food from exhausted soil, or waiting out their lives in decaying coal towns. They are among the twenty per cent of the rural U. S. population considered impoverished by the Department of Commerce in 1966 (a sharp drop from the forty per cent in 1959). In the decade from 1950-60, while employment in the rest of the country rose fifteen per cent, in Appalachia it went down by one-and-a-half per cent.

As a "pocket of poverty," Appalachia is oversized and torn by despair. Children leave school two years earlier than city children; the average adult has a sixth-grade education. Hunger and disease are rampant. One out of every four houses needs major repairs. While the nation prospers, Appalachia survives on surplus food stamps, welfare allotments, and Federal aid at the rate of $200 to $250 million a year. "The rest of the country gets automobiles and the gadgets of affluence," said a poverty worker in Tennessee. "All this region gets is silicosis."

Appalachia, rich in natural resources—coal, timber, natural gas, copper, zinc—has been brutally exploited. When deep coal mines ceased to be economically productive, the industry turned to highly automated surface strip mining, shearing entire mountainsides of trees and topsoil and leaving many thousands of miners unemployed. Water supplies are ample, but most of it is unharnessed and frequently causes floods, while four thousand miles of rivers and streams run red with mine acid drainage. Accessible stands of forest have been leveled by lumber companies; other forest land remains beyond the reach of adequate road systems. The mountain scenery is some of the most beautiful in the East, but without tourist facilities the potential is wasted.

The more venturesome—or desperate—citizens of Appalachia pack cardboard suitcases and head for Chicago or Detroit or the Army. In a decade, two and a half million have drifted away, draining communities of their best young men and leaving families without their children. "We're expected to scrape by like dogs," a fiery West Virginia ex-coal miner told Harvard psychiatrist Robert Coles. "It gets to your mind after a while. You feel as low as can be, and nervous about everything. That's what a depression does—makes you dead broke, with a lot of bills and the lowest spirits you can ever picture a man having. Sometimes I get up and I'm ready to go over to an undertaker and tell him to do something with me real fast." This miner has five children and wants them all to quit the mountains.

In their deprivation the people remain disspirited.

Cooperation between Federal and state governments has brought at best some improvement in basic physical facilities—roads, schools, hospitals, sewage disposal plants—to encourage industry and erect a solid base for higher incomes, permanent jobs, and new investment. At the same time, backwoods towns and communities judged to have no discernible potential for economic development are bypassed. Policy dictates that they be speeded toward collapse and burial. The region's projected twenty-three-hundred-mile highway network, for example, will run chiefly on a north-south axis along the mountains, ignoring many rural areas and hillside hamlets in which families live in decrepit shacks, and where the twisting, narrow, old roads still turn to mud in heavy rains. Nevertheless, even misery is relative, and in parts of the countryside, life is a little better lately. "The bare gut essentials are now being met," Tom Gish, an outspoken newspaper editor in eastern Kentucky, told a visiting reporter. "By and large people are getting fed and getting coal for the winter. If you go back to the early Sixties when there was mass hunger and violence, then you can say there's been improvement. Peace has been restored."

Along with developing the physical resources of Appalachia, the aid program has also sought to rescue its human potential—against similarly formidable odds. Political power in the mountains has traditionally been wielded by local machines which have been entrenched for decades and often regard any change—or improvement—as a threat to their continued control. Among the people themselves—living in widely scattered small communities and linked by powerful ties of kinship—proud independence and a suspicion of strangers frequently go hand in hand. Young members of VISTA (Volunteers in Service to America), organizers of Com-

munity Action Programs, and such private groups as the Appalachian Volunteers were not always welcomed. In Pike County, Kentucky, for example, three community organizers who tried to mobilize residents against further strip mining were indicted by a grand jury under a state sedition law. The grand jury declared that the volunteers "collaborated and cooperated with known communist organizers to help them organize and promote the violent overthrow of the constitutional government of Pike County." (The sedition law was later declared unconstitutional by a Federal court.)

Despite such obstacles, Community Action Programs have established rural cooperatives, built community centers, trained people to work in nursery schools, helped to start small craft industries. The Job Corps and the Neighborhood Youth Corps, together with new vocational schools, have given thousands of young people new industrial skills. Jobless fathers, called "happy pappies," now work for $1.25 an hour, repairing roads and planting trees on eroded hillsides. The arrival of new industry has slowed, and in some places reversed, the migratory flow to the cities.

But such signs of progress co-exist with a pervasive poverty now in its third generation. The flow of refugees continues, from rural poverty to urban slum. For migrating whites, the transition is hard but statistically more than three times likelier of success than that of migrating Negroes. As one Federal official declared in a report to Congress: "The tragedy that occurred in the slums of Los Angeles…began as a depression on the farm. Fundamentally, it was not a 'race riot'—but rather an explosion growing out of the poverty and despair of rural people lost in an urban slum existence that had eroded away whatever social capabilities and discipline they had at the start."

The poet Langston Hughes had previously arrived at a similar diagnosis:

What happens to a dream deferred?
Does it dry up
like a raisin in the sun?
Or fester like a sore —
And then run?
Does it stink like rotten meat?
Or crust and sugar over —
like a syrupy sweet?

Maybe it just sags
like a heavy load.

Or does it explode?

Most of the urban poor live in the ghettoes of New York, Chicago, Detroit, Los Angeles, Cleveland, Philadelphia, and other industrial centers of the nation. Whether the ghettoes are called Harlem, Watts, or Hough, they are depressingly alike. Here, said the Report of the National Advisory Commission on Civil Disorders, "segregation and poverty have intersected to destroy opportunity and hope and to enforce failure. The ghettoes too often mean men and women without jobs, families without men, and schools where children are processed instead of educated, until they return to the street — to crime, to narcotics, to dependency on welfare, and to bitterness and resentment against society in general and white society in particular." Negroes feel themselves powerless, frustrated, and surrounded by a climate of violence in which local police, often tolerant of violence, are ineffective. In Chicago, for example, rates of violent crime in a low-income, black section were thirty-five times the rate in a white, upper-class section, and seven times the rate in a white, middle-class neighborhood. White demands for "law and order" have become a cruel taunt to Negroes who want law and order most of all, since they are by far the most frequent victims of criminality.

By every yardstick, including the incidence of crime in their streets, Negroes are severely disadvantaged. Unemployment in the ghetto is about twice the rate for the white population. Even though the number of Negroes with better-paying and more secure managerial and professional jobs rose by fifty per cent between 1960 and 1966 (compared to a thirteen per cent increase for whites), Negro income on the average is still about one-half the income of whites. The annual cost of welfare is about $8 billion, but it reaches just eight million poor; forty per cent of them are Negroes, though Negroes comprise eleven per cent of the total population. Progress in housing has been slow. In 1960, thirty-six per cent of non-white males finished high school; by 1966, the ratio had climbed to fifty-three per cent (compared to seventy-three per cent for white males). But worse job opportunities for Negroes undercut the statistical improvement. One out of four Negro youths is unemployed, which led Negro moderate Bayard Rustin to ask: "What is this foolishness about training? You can't train any segment of the population unless there's a demand for their work." For a majority of the Negro poor (about sixty per cent) who are under twenty-one years of age, the limit of tolerance for continued poor law enforcement, poor jobs, poor schools, poor housing has been approaching, and with alarming speed. As Rustin said, "Impoverished, segregated and ignored Negroes [learned] that the only way they can get the ear of America is to rise up in violence."

The first serious rising of recent years broke out in 1963 in Birmingham, Alabama, where police turned dogs, cattle prods, and firehoses on Negro marchers. White racists used guns and bombs against Negroes, who retaliated by setting fire to white-owned businesses in Negro neighborhoods. One Sunday morning a bomb exploded in a Negro church, killing four young girls. Beginning in the spring of 1964 and continuing sporadically through the spring of 1968, hardly a major city in the nation was left unscarred by the wave of rioting, shooting, and fire bombing. Whether it was the accidental death of a young white civil rights activist-minister in Cleveland, the shooting of a Negro boy in New York, the arrest of a young Negro driver for speeding in Watts, or a police raid on an after-hours drinking club in Detroit — the immediate cause hardly seemed to matter. Kenneth Clark called the riots a form of "community suicide"—a self-destructive expression of hopelessness and Negro self-hatred. Others attributed the riots not to self-hatred, but to an assertion of identity, a long-suppressed aggressive rage that finally exploded. Whatever the psychological cause, urban violence seems to have become part of the American way of life.

The ingredients had been present for generations. "What white Americans have never fully understood—but what the Negro can never forget—" the Commission on Racial Disorders declared, "is that white society is deeply implicated in the ghetto. White institutions created it, white institutions maintain it, and white society condones it." The report was widely praised for its candor; many white liberals felt appropriately guilty but considered the war in Vietnam a more urgent cause for protest.

The ghetto poor got the message, however: If white America would not act on the Commission's indictment, black America would. A mood of defiance stirred a great many Negroes, organized for the first time in Community Action Programs initiated by the Office of Economic Opportunity. They held rent strikes, school strikes, welfare strikes. The entire welfare structure, from the administration of the bureaucracy to the qualifying systems of "means tests," came under attack by the poor, supported by growing numbers of academic experts who proposed an entirely new set of suggestions, including a guaranteed minimum income for everyone.

An Alabama-born woman, living in a rat-ridden Boston slum, described the tempo of protest in a conversation with the psychiatrist Robert Coles: "Up here the colored man lets it all out of his system, that what I believe. They been beating on him and lynching him ever since the beginning, and he goes from South to North and feels he can talk back, the young colored do. I try to tell my kids to be good and watch their behavior, but they don't listen. They're not afraid, like I was. They've gone from Alabama, they say, and I'm still there, they tell me."

Haggard Hollow.
The grip of Appalachian
poverty marks
the children of a neglected
Kentucky hill town.
Pictures by Charles Harbutt.

44

Brooklyn, New York

The City.
Raucous, dingy,
and dangerous,
it breaks all promises
of a better life
for the
disadvantaged.

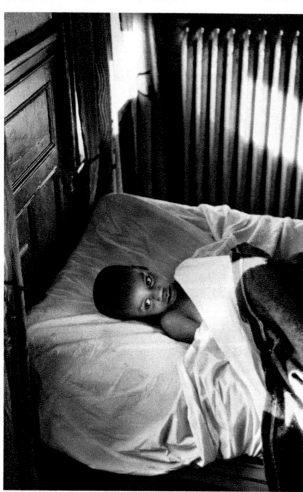

Boston, Massachusetts

58

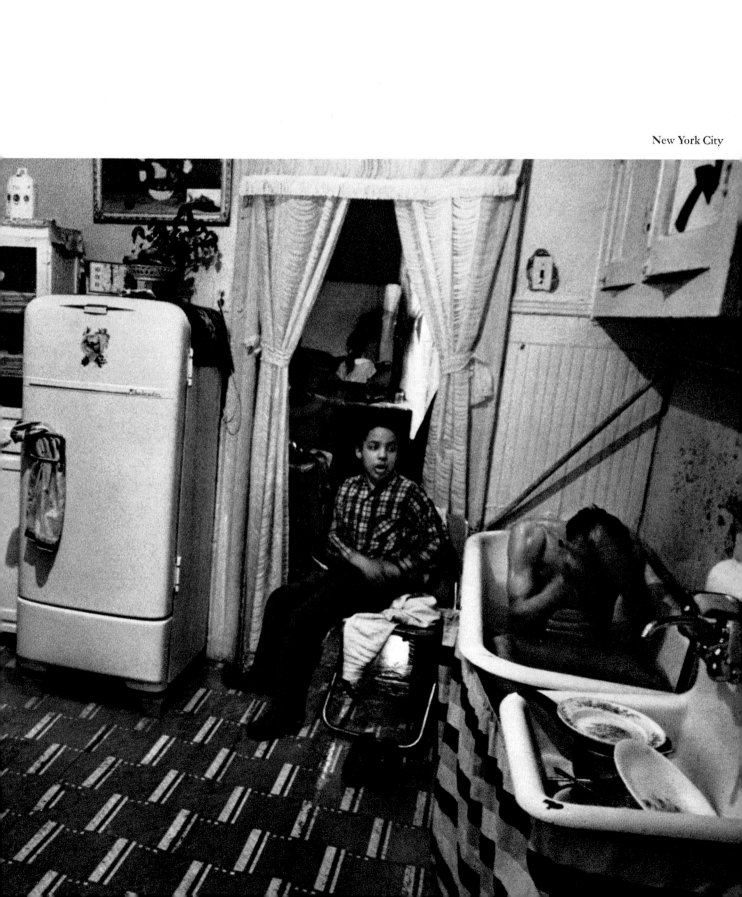

New York City: Harlem schools

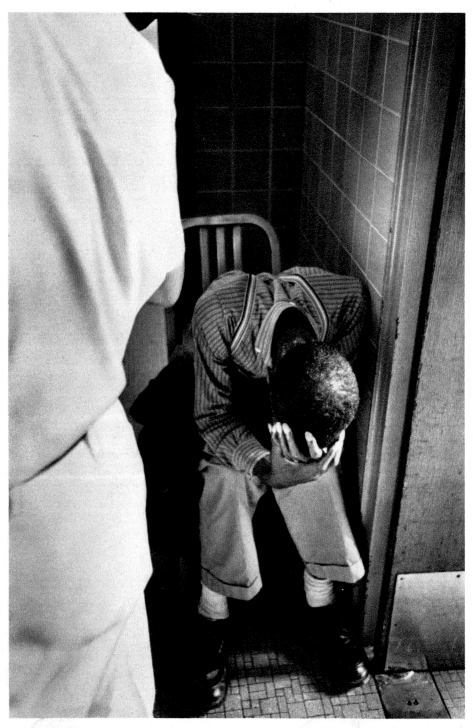

New York City: Hospital

Battle for Equality

The old civil rights movement belongs to that recent past when we spoke easily of brotherhood. It sought equal treatment for Negroes in public accommodations, polling booths, jobs, schools, housing—rights which were most blatantly denied in the South, although later protected by law and guaranteed in the courts. The movement was an interracial alliance of clergymen, middle-class professionals, intellectuals, college students, a few union leaders, and big-city Democrats. Recruited chiefly in the North, they waged civil war peacefully except when gangs of rednecks shot and killed uppity Negroes or revived the lynching bee.

The struggle for racial justice now goes under another name: the Negro Revolt, which rests on new coalitions in which whites have become outsiders. Some white liberals, drawing on their years of financial and tactical support for civil rights as if on a bank account, resentfully accuse the Negro of ingratitude. Others, made fearful by cries of revenge from the black lunatic fringe, have turned away from liberalism to engage in living-room racism: Negroes want too much too fast, they say. Between the extremes of white fear and black rage, less paranoid members of both races occupy a no-man's-land of common sense, bombarded by suspicion, hostility, and salvos of invective.

The Negro Revolt was foreshadowed by an inconspicuous and unplanned act. On the night of December 1, 1955, Rosa Parks, a Negro seamstress, refused to give up her seat to a white man on a Montgomery, Alabama, bus. She was quickly arrested and in retaliation Negro leaders of Montgomery decided to boycott the bus line. By the time a court order desegregating the buses ended the boycott, three hundred and eighty-two days later, Mrs. Parks' tired feet had set in motion a civil rights campaign that won greater gains in a decade than Negroes had achieved in the previous hundred years. The boycott also thrust leadership upon Rev. Martin Luther King, Jr., then a new minister in town. He soon became a national celebrity, the most influential civil rights theorist since Booker T. Washington and W. E. B. DuBois, and the most stirring speaker since the Negro abolitionist Frederick Douglass aroused the sympathy of northern whites before the Civil War.

Within five years of his triumph in Montgomery, King was rebuffed by Negro activists in the Student Nonviolent Coordinating Committee (SNCC), the organization of young Negroes and whites that shook up the South with a series of sit-ins during the spring and winter of 1960. Although King had been one of SNCC's founders, the activists broke with him on the ground that he was too cautious. This split marked the start of the Negro Revolt.

The student strategy of direct action quickly spread to the North, winning allies among members of the old-line National Association for the Advancement of Colored People (NAACP) and revitalizing such groups as the Congress of Racial Equality (CORE), which staged a series of Freedom Rides to Mississippi and Alabama to dramatize the segregation of interstate bus facilities. The anthem of the civil rights movement. "We Shall Overcome," whose refrain ends with the word "someday," was muffled by a new slogan, "Freedom Now." Although the 1963 March on Washington, led by King, included some fifty thousand whites among its two hundred and fifty thousand demonstrators, the trend toward Negro self-determination in the civil rights movement was unmistakable. More important, the long list of legislation initiated under the Administration of John Kennedy and carried out under Lyndon Johnson—in 1964 the poverty program and the most far-reaching civil rights bill since Reconstruction; the Voting Rights Act, Medicare, and Federal aid to education in 1965; Demonstration Cities and Fair Housing legislation in 1966 and 1968—seemed to many Negroes merely cosmetics applied to the familiar face of white racism. With some skepticism they heard President Johnson describe his Presidency as "the greatest era of American progress known since our Constitution was adopted."

The Negro was impatient, but King had faith that whites could still be moved by appeals to conscience. The strategy of nonviolent confrontation, he wrote in a famous letter from a Birmingham jail, "seeks so to dramatize the issue that it can no longer be ignored." When other Negroes looked around at the ghetto and saw that they were indeed ignored, King's influence began to wane. What Bayard Rustin called the "dignity period" of the movement had passed. Even before King's assassination, younger black militants (even the word Negro came into disfavor as an ignominious echo of the slave trade) were mocking King in private as "de Lawd." King spoke like a preacher for nonviolence and for white support in achieving wider rights, but the new leadership talked like guerrillas. They demanded basic political and economic changes, and largely ignored both the white middle class and the slowly increasing Negro middle class in favor of mobilizing the black poor. They regarded such progress as civil rights legislation a Machiavellian maneuver by whites. Apocalyptic militants approvingly quoted Frantz Fanon, a West Indian psychiatrist, whose *The Wretched of the Earth* was actually an analysis of the Algerian war: "As it develops, the war of liberation can be counted on to strike a decisive blow at the faith of the leaders. The enemy, in fact, changes his tactics. At opportune moments he combines his policy of brutal repression with spectacular gestures of friendship, maneuvers calculated to sow division...."

Even those who were willing to accept the enemy's friendly gestures at face value, recognized a new phase in the civil rights movement. "The battle for rights is over and we've won it," said Dr. James Cheek, the president of Shaw University in North Carolina. "The battle is now for equality."

The campaign promises to be long and bitter, waged in metropolitan areas that hold almost seventy per cent of the nation's Negroes. (The twelve largest cities contain over two-thirds of all Negroes outside the South and one-third of the total in the United States.) The urban ghetto population has doubled since 1950, and it is this swift demographic change that some sociologists believe to be the root cause of the current Negro fury; continuing burdens of poverty, high crime rates, drug addiction, mental illness, and other slum pathologies became unbearable. "No one can deny that all Negroes have benefitted from civil rights laws and desegregation in public life in one way or another," economist Vivian Henderson testified before the National Advisory Commission on Civil Disorders. "The fact is, however, that the masses of Negroes have not experienced tangible benefits in a significant way. This is so in education and housing. It is critically so in the area of jobs and economic security. There have been important gains but...the masses of Negroes have been virtually untouched by these gains."

Housing segregation has increased as a result of the Negro migration. Unfortunately, urban renewal often means Negro removal. Shut out of public housing by nonacceptable social patterns, some poor families are forced into worse housing than they occupied before, while the more fortunate middle-class Negroes move upward from a slum tenement to a high-rise ghetto.

Negro urbanization has also increased de facto school segregation, changing many previously mixed neighborhoods to all-black areas. "Negroes growing up in these areas," reported Thomas Pettigrew, a Harvard social psychologist, "have generally had far less equal-status contact with whites in their formative years than had Negroes of earlier generations." (Four out of five children in the U.S. attend schools that are at least ninety per cent white or black.) Ghetto schools are demonstrably worse —less competently staffed and less adequately equipped despite their need for particularly good teachers, more imaginative programs, and better equipment to help overcome the traumas of poverty, discrimination, and family disruption. Eighth-grade graduates of ghetto elementary schools commonly read at sixth-grade level, and some evidence suggests that the schools themselves contribute to these failures. A serious decline in test scores generally begins in the third grade and increases with each year of schooling.

Better-paying industrial jobs, largely controlled by organized labor in big cities, have been denied to many residents of the ghetto. Negroes have been cabinet members, ambassadors, Federal judges, and big-city mayors, but only 2.7 per cent of union-controlled apprenticeships are filled by Negroes— an increase of one per cent in ten years. In 1966, a four-city U.S. Labor Department survey of union plumbers, steam fitters, sheet metal workers, stone masons, structural iron workers, operating engineers, lathers, painters, glaziers, and asbestos workers failed to disclose a *single* Negro apprentice. It is easier for a Negro to enter an Ivy League college than to join some craft unions.

Yet the very fact that it is now easier to enter college, find an office job, work as a community organizer, or vote for a Negro who is running for office (more than seven hundred Negroes hold elective posts) has had a disruptive impact on Negro life. The poorly educated and unskilled grow more despairing and resentful. The better educated, with wider opportunities to join the prospering Negro middle class, become more frustrated. As a Negro poverty worker in Detroit explained the effect of the city's "Golden Door" to a reporter: "In Jackson, Mississippi, no Negro can get through the door and strangely enough that can be kind of reassuring. He can always say it's a white door and so there's no use a black man even trying. Some call it Negro laziness or apathy, but it's the disease of the ghetto. In Detroit the door is open—at least to the prepared Negro and even to some half-prepared ones. The guy who doesn't get through no longer can find solace in saying, 'I can't make it because I'm black.' He has to face the black pain."

Out of such pain, out of the general white indifference to it, and out of the belief that Negroes must fashion their own success instead of having marginal gains "conferred" upon them was born a new Negro credo. "Black Power" was first heard as a chant on James Meredith's one-man "march against fear" from Memphis to Jackson, Mississippi, in June, 1966. Initially it sounded a mood, not a program. Other slogans like it—"black consciousness," "Black is Beautiful"—encouraged racial pride, replacing the sense of inferiority and self-hatred fostered by white supremacists and, in the view of young militants, well-meaning liberals also. Quickly, however, black power did become a program— many programs, in fact, whose meanings and objectives were hotly debated by whites and Negroes. In politics it came to mean independent political action, organizing the voting power of the ghetto, increasing voter registration in the rural South, pressuring for redrawing of election district boundaries, nominating black political leaders who owed whites nothing. To some, black political power meant little more than "bloc power," a historic factor in ethnic voting. The economic meaning of black power similarly grew out of the mood of independence and deepening racial solidarity. The ghetto should be run by local businessmen, not "exploited" by absentee white owners. In education as in other white-run ghetto institutions—hospitals, police, housing—black power demands local control and a chance for Negroes to determine their own futures. Black power has shown up in fashion; African dress and natural hair styles have become symbolic badges of the movement. "Black power," said professor Charles Hamilton, a political scientist and co-author of a book with Stokely Carmichael, "is concerned with organizing the rage of black people...[it] must not be naïve about the intentions of white people to yield anything without a struggle and a confrontation with organized power. Black people will gain only as much as they can win through their ability to organize independent bases of economic and political power—through boycotts, electoral activity, rent strikes, work stoppages, pressure-group bargaining."

In one sense, black power is more than a century old. Frederick Douglass said in 1848: "It is evident that we can be improved and elevated just as fast and far as we shall improve and elevate ourselves." In new and heightened rhetoric, it has been more angrily articulated by Malcolm X, the Black Muslim leader who was assassinated by enemies within the sect and whose puritanical message of self-improvement, carried out in black nationalist isolation from white society, has raised him to mythic status. Among the most extreme advocates of black power, the slogan is a call to retaliatory violence.

Such belief in violence ranges from legal right of self-defense, espoused by the Black Panthers in California and elsewhere, to justifications of looting and arson in ghetto riots, guerrilla warfare, and, in its most romantic form, armed rebellion. Doomsday visions which suggest that whites are preparing mass extermination of Negroes are understandable expressions of utter hopelessness. Yet such perceptions could turn out to be self-fulfilling prophecies. As David Riesman, a sympathetic observer, has pointed out, "The present need is for 'action,' at least as an occupational therapy. This leads to charisma without an object, to revolutionary tactics without a revolutionary situation, to revolutionary rhetoric that may in turn bring about a new and even deeper cynicism and nihilism."

Just as Frederick Douglass' insistence on Negro control of Negro destiny is part of the people's history, so is the current attack on integration as a means of achieving equality. While none has gone as far as Marcus Garvey's "back to Africa" movement of fifty years ago, separatist arguments are in vogue as assertions of black identity. The Reverend Albert Cleague, Jr., of Detroit, whose congregation prays to a black Madonna and who has organized the Black Star Cooperative, has declared: "If you're waiting for the white man to love you, to reach down and help you, drop dead. As long as you believe in integration, there's no place for you but on your knees." And to Robert S. Browne, who teaches economics to white college students, "the 'accepted' Negro, the 'integrated' Negro, are mere euphemisms which hide a cruel and relentless cultural destruction." Browne does not suggest that blacks return to Africa, but proposes instead a formal partitioning of the United States into separate nations of whites and blacks.

As the result of the debate over black power,

conservative Negro organizations have become more militant. The National Urban League, which undertakes to secure jobs for Negroes in white firms, and is thus somewhat dismayed by inflamed Negro rhetoric, nevertheless not only adopted "black power" as a slogan of "pride and community solidarity," but pronounced two new slogans: "Soul Power" and "Ghetto Power." At the same time, the Urban League remained old-fashioned enough to criticize separatism. "We do not intend to do the racists' job for them by accepting segregation," said Whitney Young, Jr., the League's executive director. With greater fervor, the other major entrenched civil rights organization, the NAACP, called on Negroes to publicly denounce "extremists who are shrilly and insistently espousing apartheid; racism, including anti-Semitism; intimidation and violence....The time has come to speak out loud and clear lest the entire race be branded as hatemongers, segregationists, advocates of violence and worse."

In their view of the world beyond the ghetto, Negro militants and moderates also disagreed. The traditional leadership—with the notable exception of Martin Luther King—was inclined to accept the existing political and economic system of the United States, and avoided an organizational stand on Vietnam which could further alienate white support for the Negro cause. Black militant groups such as SNCC and the Panthers, and speakers such as Stokely Carmichael and Eldridge Cleaver, condemned the war as an example of "imperialist genocide" against a nonwhite population. The Vietnamese were considered political soul brothers, victimized by a society said to be irredeemably corrupt and racist. The ideological argument was sharpened by the casualty figures. Although Negroes make up eleven per cent of the population, and represented

only 12.6 per cent of Army personnel in Vietnam between 1961 and 1966, they accounted for more than twenty per cent of the fatalities. Nevertheless, the rate of re-enlistment for Negroes in 1966, when casualties in Vietnam spurted upward, was 66.5 per cent, more than three times the rate for whites. On this basis, Carmichael asserted that the war was a device by whites "to get rid of black people in the ghettoes."

To many blacks, however, the Army is the best and perhaps the only escape from poverty and the ghetto. Though traces of discrimination persist, it is probably the most integrated institution in America. Yet the same factors which attract many Negroes into the Army and lead them to re-enlist also account for their over-representation in the front lines. Lacking education and skills, they join up; lacking education and skills, they make excellent candidates for the infantry. Also, many Negroes volunteer for elite, high casualty fighting units which pay higher salaries.

Last year, according to one estimate, about five thousand black veterans of Vietnam returned home intact. Contrary to the hopes of some black nationalists, they did not rush forward to grab guns. On the other hand, their integrated Army experience may have made them more aware of civilian discrimination. The reflections of one returning soldier who found a $7,500-a-year job within a few weeks of his discharge are probably typical. "A black G.I. coming back from Vietnam can't help feeling strongly about the situation here," he said. "Don't be deceived that just because he gets a job that he isn't going to get involved. The important thing is that he's coming back to the same old stuff. Just helping a man get a job isn't going to erase the bitterness and sense of injustice. It is a step in the right direction, but it isn't the answer."

Selma, Alabama

South Carolina: Ku Klux Klan members

Birmingham, Alabama

Selma, Alabama

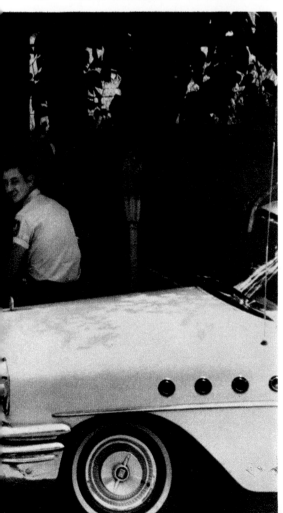

73

Mississippi: Policeman's obscene gesture to Freedom Marchers

Selma, Alabama

Washington, D.C., riot

Memphis, Tennessee

The Unwanted War

At first it was not a war, not even a "police action" like Korea, and only wild men thought the United States should mobilize an army to fight in Vietnam. In 1954, when the French defeat was imminent, President Eisenhower warned that he "could conceive of no greater tragedy than for the United States to become involved in an all-out war in Indochina." In 1963 President Kennedy said: "In the final analysis, it is their war.... We can help them, we can give them equipment, we can send our men out there as advisers, but they have to win it—the people of Vietnam—against the Communists." Lyndon B. Johnson also preached restraint and seemed to recognize the risk of widening the war. During the 1964 campaign he told the nation that "I want to be very cautious when I start dropping bombs around that are likely to involve American boys in a war in Asia with seven hundred million Chinese." Two weeks before the election he declared: "We are not about to send American boys nine thousand or ten thousand miles away from home to do what Asian boys should be doing for themselves." At the time, about eighteen thousand American "advisers" were in Vietnam.

Almost imperceptibly "their" war became ours, and not only militarily. Like a great thundercloud, Vietnam darkened the American mood and cast its shadow everywhere—on campuses and churches, farms and ghettoes, and finally on the White House. Once considered expendable, Vietnam became a pivotal test of honor; to retreat, the Government said, would invite "another Munich." Though for years the struggle had been considered basically a civil war, in 1965 it was officially redefined as an aggressive invasion. "In an important sense," said a former State Department official, Vietnam assumed crucial significance "because we have said it is of crucial significance." With every escalation of rhetoric came a matching escalation of men, money, and equipment to justify the new policy declarations.

By the end of 1968, with half a million American troops and huge quantities of matériel in Vietnam, the war was costing the United States $30 billion a year. In seven years thirty-one thousand American soldiers have died, one hundred thousand have been seriously wounded. Civilian casualties in South Vietnam are estimated at between one hundred thousand and one hundred and fifty thousand a year; hundreds of thousands of Vietnamese are hungry and homeless, and at least two million refugees have fled from the countryside to the cities. Lyndon Johnson avoided the ultimate tragedy; he once confided to a daughter: "Your Daddy may go down in history as having unleashed World War III." But by almost every other yardstick the war was a disaster.

The enormous American buildup prevented a Vietcong victory, but it was far from insuring a Vietcong defeat. The advantages of massive U.S. firepower were whittled away in a war without conventional front lines, with few large-scale battles, and waged over cruel terrain. Repeatedly, "search and destroy" missions against the Vietcong guerrillas came back empty-handed. The enemy slipped through the traps and little was left to destroy except the hamlets which may have harbored them. During daylight, ground sweeps and incessant bombing kept the Vietcong on the defensive. At night the land belonged to them. The bombing of the North, which was expected to bring Hanoi to its knees, also proved futile. In 1965, when the bombing began in earnest, there were about five thousand North Vietnamese in the South; three years and seven hundred thousand tons of explosives later, there were well over one hundred thousand. The anticipated psychological effect of the bombing proved illusory. The Tet offensive, simultaneously launched in Saigon and a dozen other major cities in February, 1968, demonstrated that Hanoi had ample will power, as well as manpower, in reserve.

While the war dragged on, ravaging the countryside, an atmosphere of cynicism permeated the cities where the wealthier Vietnamese, if they could not profit from the war, did their best to ignore it. Vainly did the United States urge a succession of Saigon leaders, starting with Ngo Dinh Diem, to make the social reforms essential to win mass support. Refusing to be American "puppets," they danced to strings pulled by the same privileged few who traditionally manipulated the country's political life. A government which feared fundamental change not surprisingly turned out to be the largest obstacle to it. The South Vietnamese Army, charged with protecting peasant villagers and fostering loyalty to the central Government, failed on both counts. Except in a few secure areas, hamlets were never free from guerrilla attack. Peasants remained apathetic or hostile; their only contact with Saigon was the exorbitant rent they paid to absentee landlords. Political rule was ineffective. Corruption and nepotism remained the twin pillars of government, puncturing democratic pretensions and undermining the army's effectiveness. Land reform, the country's most urgent need, was routinely sabotaged or stymied; with two per cent of the landlords clinging to forty-five per cent of the land, peasants rarely got land or reform. And without the sense of hope and commitment that political and social progress might bring, the war itself was a huge but largely misspent effort. The most ambitious political experiment was the national election held in the fall of 1967. The Saigon Government won only one-third of the vote, although it had the open support of the armed forces, the advantage of incumbency, and an opposition slate of candidates whose programs offered no serious alternatives. (Opponents who might have proposed far-reaching domestic reforms or de-escalation of the war were in jail or otherwise barred from running.) The Government obviously was not overwhelmingly popular, but it was the only one we had—a dilemma which reporter Neil Sheehan summed up in *The New York Times* Magazine: "We shall, I am afraid, have to put up with our Vietnamese mandarin allies. We shall not be able to reform them and it is unlikely that we shall be able to find any other Vietnamese willing to cooperate with us...." A Marine Corps officer who retired in order to write a book on Vietnam stated the issue even more bluntly. Former Lt. Col. William Corson wrote in *The Betrayal:* "The common rationalizations to justify the need of a totalitarian government during wartime do not hold when it comes to the Government of Vietnam. It has done nothing right. There is nothing to commend it."

Such flat statements were open to dispute, but not much. In the United States, Administration supporters urged more patience, a higher military investment, and greater sacrifice to prove to the communists that so-called "wars of national liberation" could not pay off. But as the limited war grew wider and costlier with no end in sight, the problem of Vietnam agonized the policymakers, baffled public opinion, and divided the nation with bitter antagonism. Occasionally accusing dissenters of walking the edge of disloyalty, leading political figures asserted that peace marches and other antiwar demonstrations only encouraged the enemy to fight harder, thus prolonging the bloody struggle. "Whose side are they on?" the Secretary of State demanded to know. Such testy questions, hinting at Administration reprisals, managed only to inflame debate. If free discussion is the essence of democracy, said political scientist Hans Morgenthau, dissenters cannot remain silent. "If there is nobody to tell the truth as he sees it—truth that diverges from the official line—there would never be the possibility of correcting error," Morgenthau said, "because then power and truth are identical until disaster corrects that mistake. That was what happened in Nazi Germany." Some dissenters argued that the war was immoral and/or unwinnable and called for quick negotiations to extricate the United States from the hopeless cause. Others sympathized openly or discreetly with the Vietcong and urged immediate and unilateral withdrawal. Never did the objectives of a major U.S. war seem more ambiguous or more fiercely contested. Richard M. Nixon was no dove but a realist when, in October, 1967, he recognized that "the war has imposed severe strains on the United States, not just militarily and economically but socially and politically as well. Bitter dissension has torn the fabric of American intellectual life and whatever the outcome of the war, the tear may be a long time mending."

If Vietnam was a cause of national travail, the protests were a symptom of deep national anxiety and frustration. Long submerged, these finally broke through the surface tension created by the war, inspiring far-ranging questioning of traditional policy aims at home and overseas.

Since the end of World War II foreign policy had been dictated by a cold war script. But Red China's break with the Soviet Union, coupled with the rise of national communism in Eastern Europe, made obsolete the stereotype of an international conspiracy housed in the Kremlin. Moreover, the obvious desire of the United States and the Soviets to avoid a nuclear showdown clamped further restraints on foreign adventures that might lead to such a confrontation. In this context, Vietnam was the first crisis of the post-cold-war era. As a continuation of a twenty-year struggle against French colonialism, it did not belong on that familiar ideological battleground between "the free world" and communism. Instead, Vietnam revealed that American military power alone could not impose political solutions in revolutionary situations and strongly suggested that Washington's role as the world's policeman needed rethinking.

It was often said that the war drained the country's domestic energy and resources, diverting attention from crucial internal needs. The cities were becoming unmanageable. The ghettoes were already unlivable. For youthful activists, the few years of hope in the early Sixties had faded, turning to disappointment, estrangement, and unrest. Among radicals, the conventional notions of individual liberty and political compromise were scorned in favor of "revolutionary justice" ("Up against the wall") and absolutist politics. Among Negroes the same sense of let-down prompted the same impulse to revolt. But Congress seemed satisfied with the existing priorities. Judging by the allocations of money and manpower, Washington preferred waging the unpopular war in Vietnam to the even more unpopular war on poverty.

Many of those who did not openly protest the war nevertheless held profound misgivings. For some, Vietnam became a moral question: On what should America spend its affluence? For others, particularly the young, the war was a question of life itself. "Never before in our history has a war been fought with so little involvement by the society as a whole," conceded John Roche, former

White House adviser, who supported Presidential policy. "Which is another way of saying that Vietnam really has been an adult's war and a young man's fight." Which is also why the first major protests against the war took place on college campuses. First at the University of Michigan, then in dozens of other schools, faculty and students organized marathon "teach-ins"—twenty-four hours of speeches, seminars, and song. To give the occasion an academic veneer, Government speakers were also invited, though few appeared. For some students, protest was touched with guilt since they could object to the war with impunity granted by draft deferments. Overcoming self-interest, however, many undergraduates pressured universities to abolish class rankings used by local draft boards to decide deferment. Several leading institutions eliminated class standings entirely, while others transmitted the rankings directly to students, letting them decide what to do.

Academic opposition to the war was most intense in the humanities and the social sciences. As the most articulate campus groups, they were very effective critics. Richard Rovere, whose book *Waist Deep in the Big Muddy* was an eloquent and sober condemnation of the war, summed up the prevailing intellectual climate. "This is the first war of the century," he wrote, "of which it is true that opposition to it is not only widespread but fashionable."

Increasing numbers of prominent clergymen joined the dissenters, and as the protests gained momentum objection became more respectable. The middle class became more uneasy. During a "Spring Mobilization for Peace" march in 1967, a crowd estimated at between one hundred thousand and four hundred thousand from the eastern United States gathered in Central Park in New York City.

On the same day on the West Coast, sixty thousand people staged a protest in San Francisco. Some militants waved Vietcong flags, some were hippies, but large numbers were middle-aged and elderly; married couples pushed baby carriages and young businessmen paraded with ties pushed neatly to the collar. Probably the most dramatic tableau of the peace movement was a two-day march on Washington in October, 1967, by at least one hundred thousand demonstrators. The finale, a vigil at the steps of the Pentagon, began peacefully but ended with violence, mass arrests, and the lingering fumes of tear gas. "It is not wild-eyed idealism but clear-eyed revulsion that brings us here," said the chaplain of Yale, William Sloane Coffin. "For as one of our number put it: 'If what the United States is doing in Vietnam is right, what is there left to be called wrong?'" Two months later Coffin, pediatrician Benjamin Spock, and three others were indicted for conspiring to counsel young men to violate the draft law. They were convicted, and appealed their case to the U.S. Supreme Court.

Support for the war continued to sag, but the intensity of the fighting increased. It was almost as though the picketing and the protests had been meaningless. Within the peace movement a new slogan was born—"From dissent to resistance"—resulting in such protests as nonpayment of income taxes, burning draft cards in public ceremonies, napalming selective service records, and hurling balloons filled with urine and animal blood at Cabinet officers. The tactical shift from peaceful civil disobedience was criticized as revolutionary exhibitionism, but it polarized much public opinion just the same. By then few politicians could shrug off antiwar sentiment as the work of hairy kids or grown-up communist sympathizers. And though only a handful of men in the United States Senate would have voted to end the war, every member realized that public opinion back home had swung considerably against the war policy. Not since April, 1966, had the President enjoyed majority support in the polls, and the percentage had been dropping steadily since then.

The climate of gloom was suddenly transformed into political action by Senator Eugene McCarthy, an urbane and somewhat aloof former college professor. McCarthy announced his decision to oppose the President for the nomination in late November. Earlier that month he had told an audience of young Democrats that it was time for political leaders to join academics, clergymen, and students in publicly demanding an end to the war. "This is not the kind of political controversy," he said, "which should be left to a children's crusade or to those not directly involved in politics." Fellow Democrats did not leap to his support. It was a children's crusade of five thousand college students that got out the vote in New Hampshire in March, a primary election which demonstrated the depth of public dismay over Vietnam. McCarthy won more than forty-two per cent of the vote, confounding the pollsters and surprising many of his own supporters.

Immediately on hearing the result, Senator Robert Kennedy, who a month earlier had decided not to split the Democratic Party by opposing Lyndon Johnson, changed his mind and entered the battle for the nomination. Two weeks later, with politics in turmoil and with his popularity down to a record low of twenty-six per cent, the President abruptly renounced further claims on the White House. Simultaneously he ordered a stop to the bombing of most of North Vietnam. Within sixty hours Hanoi's response cleared the way to peace talks in Paris. Within sixty seconds, the road to the Democratic convention had taken an astonishing twist, and the political scene was transformed.

Although the President's withdrawal came too late to allow Hubert Humphrey the choice of entering the forthcoming series of state primary elections, the Vice President nevertheless held an overwhelming lead among party delegates. Democratic functionaries were not about to commit the sin of disloyalty, nor would they concede past error in Vietnam now that the first step toward negotiations had been taken. Robert Kennedy's political machine, primed for 1972, swung smoothly into high gear. As had John Kennedy, Robert appealed strongly to the young, the poor, and to minorities — the groups penalized most by the war and its side effects. Although it was widely assumed that the Kennedy magic and Kennedy money would soon sink the McCarthy campaign, the experts were wrong again. First to challenge the President, McCarthy's nonchalant boldness fired the imagination of idealists. Campaigning with scarcely a nod to conventional rules, and even flouting them frequently with indifference, he won supporters among those weary of the cant and clichés that routinely pass for political stumpmanship.

From the start, McCarthy offered two reasons for running: to give the public the chance "to pass judgment on the Vietnam war and on the character and priorities of this nation," and to prove, "especially to students, that the democratic system still works." By the end of the campaign it was clear that neither proposition had been widely endorsed. The beginning of peace talks in Paris had diminished Vietnam as a campaign issue; national priorities were more actively professed than pursued; and among many of the nation's youth there was not only doubt whether the political system worked, but whether the educational system, the social system, or the value system worked, either.

District 8 / Outskirts of Saigon.
Reclaimed from swampland
and built up with U.S. aid,
it was a showplace of
pro-Government sentiment and action —
until the Tet offensive.
Pictures by Philip Jones Griffiths.

Infantry.
The faces of Americans
who fought at Hue.
Pictures by Donald McCullin.

A Soldier Returns.
The death of a young
South Carolina paratrooper
— Pfc. Harold T. Edmondson — is a
sad, irrevocable consequence
of a distressful war.
Pictures by Constantine Manos.

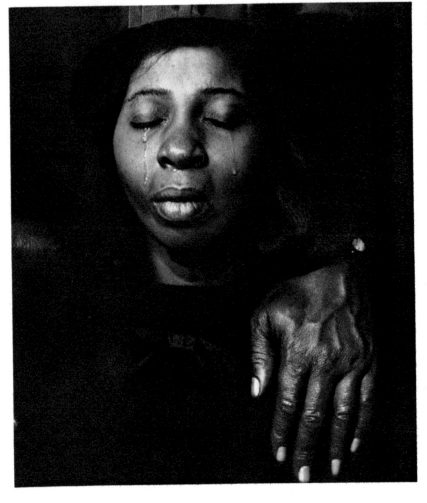

White House fence

Outcry for Peace.

Washington, D.C.

New York City: Peace march

New York City: Opposition

Washington, D.C.

The McCarthy Phenomenon.
Pictures by Charles Harbutt.

New Hampshire: Victory

New Hampshire

The Kennedy Magic.
Pictures by Burt Glinn & Cornell Capa.

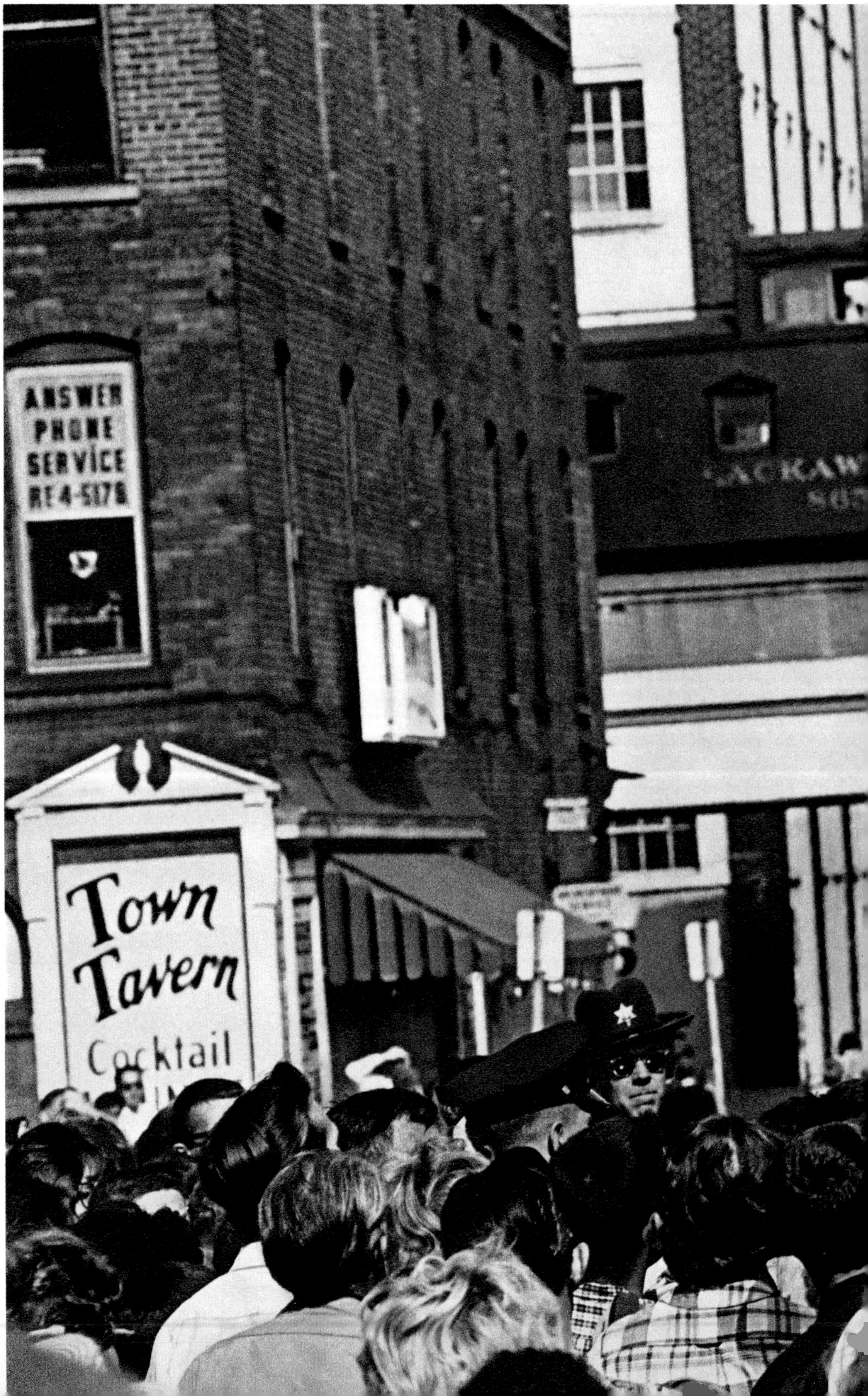
ANSWER
PHONE
SERVICE
RE 4-5178
Town
Tavern
Cocktail

Confrontation

During the summer of 1964, as delegates to the Republican Party convention hastened to the Cow Palace in San Francisco, the University of California at Berkeley was knee-deep in a rising tide of political protest. For students responding to the moral concerns pronounced by the Kennedy Administration, the overriding issue was civil rights. By the hundreds they had fanned out from the campus to the Deep South, staging demonstrations and working with Negro grass-roots organizations. Back home, putting to work the lessons learned in "the Movement," they crossed the Bay to San Francisco, picketing in support of Negro job opportunities at major stores, taking over the lobby of the Sheraton Palace for a sleep-in, and opposing the repeal of a new fair-housing law.

Conservative California politicians were incensed. They demanded a university ban against recruiting demonstrators on campus for "illegal" off-campus protests, and an end to fund-raising for political causes on school property.

When students returned for the fall term, they suddenly encountered a new regulation that prohibited recruiting and fund-raising for social and political causes on university grounds. Activists, finding a cause that many moderates could endorse, moved quickly to defy the ban. A police car dispatched to arrest a violator was surrounded by four thousand chanting students; the officers inside were held ignominiously captive for thirty-two hours. A few weeks later, mobilized under the banner of the Free Speech Movement, eight hundred students invaded the administration building for a sit-in. "The time has come to put our bodies on the machine and stop it," said Mario Savio, a leader of the revolt, as the demonstration began. "We will stay until the police remove us." They did and the police did, dragging some of the University's brightest students off to jail.

It was the beginning of the Battle of Berkeley, a struggle which for months paralyzed the campus, divided scholars into warring factions, and crystallized a national political movement of the New Left. Its goals are not merely Negro equality and "restructuring" large and often impersonal universities, but transforming all of society. In the words of Herbert Marcuse, the German-born philosopher whose views were appropriated as the theoretical basis of the apocalypse: "I have tried to show that any change would require a total rejection or, to speak the language of the students, a perpetual confrontation of this society. And that is not merely a question of changing the institutions but rather, and this is more important, of totally changing human beings in their attitudes, their instincts, their goals, and their values." Were the student missionaries humanist reformers? Certainly not reformers and not humanists, either. "According to them, humanism is a bourgeois personal value," said Marcuse.

While the moral revolutionaries of Berkeley set out to pursue social justice, sometimes by means that critics looked upon as antisocial and unjust, another group of young pioneers was settling across the Bay in a run-down section of San Francisco known as Haight-Ashbury. The hippies were the advance guard of a new drug subculture for which politics meant nothing and for whom psychedelia, love, and personal freedom were everything. "Lucy may be in the Sky with Diamonds," said the historian J. H. Plumb, "but it is the Negro in the ghetto who matters." Hippies disagreed. The real world could go hang while they did their "own thing." It was a credo with much appeal to youth concerned with identity, and it quickly spread from the pads of the Hashbury to East Coast suburbia.

Direct action and drugs, protest and privatism,

are the responses of a generation which many regard as not just inexperienced and romantic ("The trouble with youth," as Irvin S. Cobb said, "is that it hasn't read the minutes of the last meeting"), but precociously experienced and shrewdly realistic. Middle-class children of privilege, they are not rebelling traditionally against parents (though the tradition has not been wholly forgotten); they are rebelling in favor of the vision that liberal parents once held, then beclouded and abandoned. Defiance of authority—church, state, and institutional—has a long and honorable history in America and the young are passionately renewing it. Unreasonable about what is "reasonable"—personal compromise, creature comforts, social inequities—activists protest what Kenneth Keniston has called "the institutionalization of hypocrisy," the difference between ideals and realities which most societies silently ignore.

On the other side of the generation gap, adult reaction, on the whole, was remarkably tolerant. Although some adults launched their own attack against youth's moralism and zeal—which only reinforced the younger generation's determination to correct the waywardness of their elders—not a few grown-ups in the academies and elsewhere ventured to build bridges to the other side. Perhaps the response of adults was best summed up by the man who symbolized all that rebel youth was supposed to detest. According to Daniel P. Moynihan, the "misery and puzzlement" of Lyndon B. Johnson was apparent when the President told an aide: "They are the best generation of young people we have ever had, and they are all against us."

So the gap first expressed by the civil rights struggle, then widened by war, has grown to divide the generations in ways that are both intense and unique. For youth, the past is deplorable, the present is intolerable, and the future is full of fears, including the fear that there will be no future. "We have lived through a period of depravity and insanity and finally of numbness and insensitivity," wrote Robert Allan Haber, a past president of Students for a Democratic Society (S.D.S.), the flying wedge of the amorphous New Left coalition. "Out of the memories of wars, atomic explosions, atrocities, race riots—out of a heritage of absurdity—a direct-action movement has grown. We have taken the initiative from the adult spokesmen and leadership, setting the pace and policy as our actions evolve their own dynamic. Pessimism and cynicism have given way to direct action." Hence, "Don't trust anyone over thirty" (a cry first raised at Berkeley), a blanket indictment that covers as much as it reveals.

In contrast to the radicals of the Thirties, who were ideologically oriented, worked generally from specific programs, and had the benefit of recognizable targets (communism, capitalism, fascism), today's young radicals emphasize a political style more than a political structure. They are readier to seize institutions than to plan new ones. They have retrieved "anarchy" and "nihilism" from the dustbin of history—but as slogans, not movements. This style, coupled with the younger generation's unprecedented moral energy, has given relatively small numbers of protesters great influence. Only some eight hundred draft resisters have been jailed and perhaps fifteen hundred young men have fled to Canada. Out of a national student body of seven million, only about one hundred thousand, between one and two per cent of the total, are "radical activists," according to a Harris poll in the spring of 1968. But many thousands have marched in antiwar demonstrations, protested before government buildings, and manned the barricades in a second

119

wave of campus revolts that began with another Berkeley at Columbia University and spread to dozens of schools across the country.

The occupation of several buildings at Columbia for several days by a few hundred members and followers of S.D.S. touched off a new round of academic self-analysis over the university vs. student power. It was a triumph of "confrontation politics," and proof of the university's essential defenselessness in the face of violent challenge. On hand were the dispossessed elite—students in revolt against everything from rules governing female visitors, to faculty indifference, to University research (secret and open) conducted for the Federal government. They were often joined by younger members of the teaching staff and graduate students, who had their own scores to settle with disinterested professors and a fumbling administration. Black students were moved by more immediate goals. They sought more black students and faculty, courses relevant to the black experience— objectives which did not threaten traditional university structures. Blacks thus wanted greater access to the system, while white students not only sought to radically change the system, but to use it as a launching pad for the broader attack on the "military-industrial complex" in which they saw Columbia taking an integral part. "The S.D.S. seized a building in order to wreck the University," a black student said later. "We retained a building in order to gain some power in the University."

It was a valid distinction, recognized not only among white revolutionaries but among "counter-revolutionary" professors, many of whom were once in the vanguard of the Old Left. "In the end," said Nathan Glazer, a sociologist who lived through the Berkeley chaos, "one must judge whether the student radicals fundamentally represent a better world that can come into being, or whether they are not committed to outdated and romantic visions that cannot be realized....They remind me more of the Luddite machine smashers than the Socialist trade unionists who achieved citizenship and power for workers." Sociologist Daniel Bell, who analyzed the Columbia "insurrection" at length, viewed it in a wider perspective. Throughout the advanced industrialized nations, the growing restlessness of youth was a symptom of what has been variously called the "postmodern" era, the "post-industrial" society, and the "technetronic" age. In a time of unprecedented change, basic institutions are inevitably lagging behind. In the United States, further advanced technologically than the rest of the world, the disruption occurs first and most severely. We are poised on the edge of new and complex problems of social organization for which old solutions will not work. At the same time, Bell had harsh words for the student radicals. While the old political liberalism is in crisis, he said, "the New Left, as a social movement, is passing through a phase ranging from protest to resistance to desperation....Desperado tactics are never the mark of a coherent social movement, but the guttering last gasps of a romanticism soured by rancor and impotence. It lives on turbulence but is incapable of transforming its chaotic impulses into a systematic, responsible behavior that is necessary to effect broad societal change. It is not impelled to innovation but to destruction."

Sociologists are known to disagree, however. Speaking with equal fervor, a member of the President's Commission on the Causes and Prevention of Violence defended the students against Bell's indictment. "The student generation is not a generation of 'romantics,' a charge often hurled at them," said Jerome H. Skolnick. "The older generation that waves the flag, that sees America as a country of manifest destiny saving the world for democracy —they are the romantics. The younger generation is by contrast a generation of realists who are not willing to kill or be killed unless the cause is unmistakably honorable. In this perspective, the issue today is not what is wrong with the younger generation in trying to overturn established institutions, but what is wrong with the older generations in trying to conduct business as usual....Which is preferable, the violent revolutionary act or the severe social sanctions that slowly, sometimes negligently, impinge upon masses of human beings on the basis of their racial or ethnic characteristics?"

Whichever diagnosis is correct, and the outcome is by no means certain, what group along the broad front of discontented youth can best survive? Hippiedom seems to be dying; communities preaching peace and gentleness have been stained by violence, greed, and the terror of too many bad "trips." Marijuana enjoys a growing clientele, but users seem to prefer it as an underground recreation rather than as the foundation for a new way of life. Two other groups remain, one tiny and bizarre, and one large and conventional.

The Yippies, formally the Youth International Party, mix the theory of nonviolence, the use of hallucinogens, and the politics of protest into an unstable combination. Executing their mandate that protest should be fun, Yippies showered dollar bills from the gallery of the New York Stock Exchange and nominated a live pig named Pigasus for President. "It's the politics of ecstasy," said Jerry Rubin, a Yippie leader who earned his stripes at Berkeley. "It's dancing, it's guerrilla theater."

The second group of disaffected youth occupies the conventional center. These are the hundreds of thousands of would-be organization men willing to protest within the framework of traditional politics, but now without an organization that appeals to them. They are the followers of Robert Kennedy and John Kennedy, who prodded awake a dozing college generation and for a while revived their interest in politics. They include the youths who were "clean for Gene" in New Hampshire and remained with the campaign long enough to erase the jokes about a children's crusade; rebuffed by the Democrats, many later dropped out. Most of the youthful supporters of the Kennedys and McCarthy were not members of the New Left except in the loosest sense. Heirs of the old liberalism, they believed that the system functioned—badly, to be sure, but perhaps reparable with major effort.

Then came Chicago, a televised trauma in which radicals and reformers, surrealists, tacticians, and ordinary onlookers jointly received a lesson in what is widely described as the democratic process.

THE·HEROIC·D

REVOLUT

New York City: Columbia '68 graduate

New York City: Timothy Leary in East Village

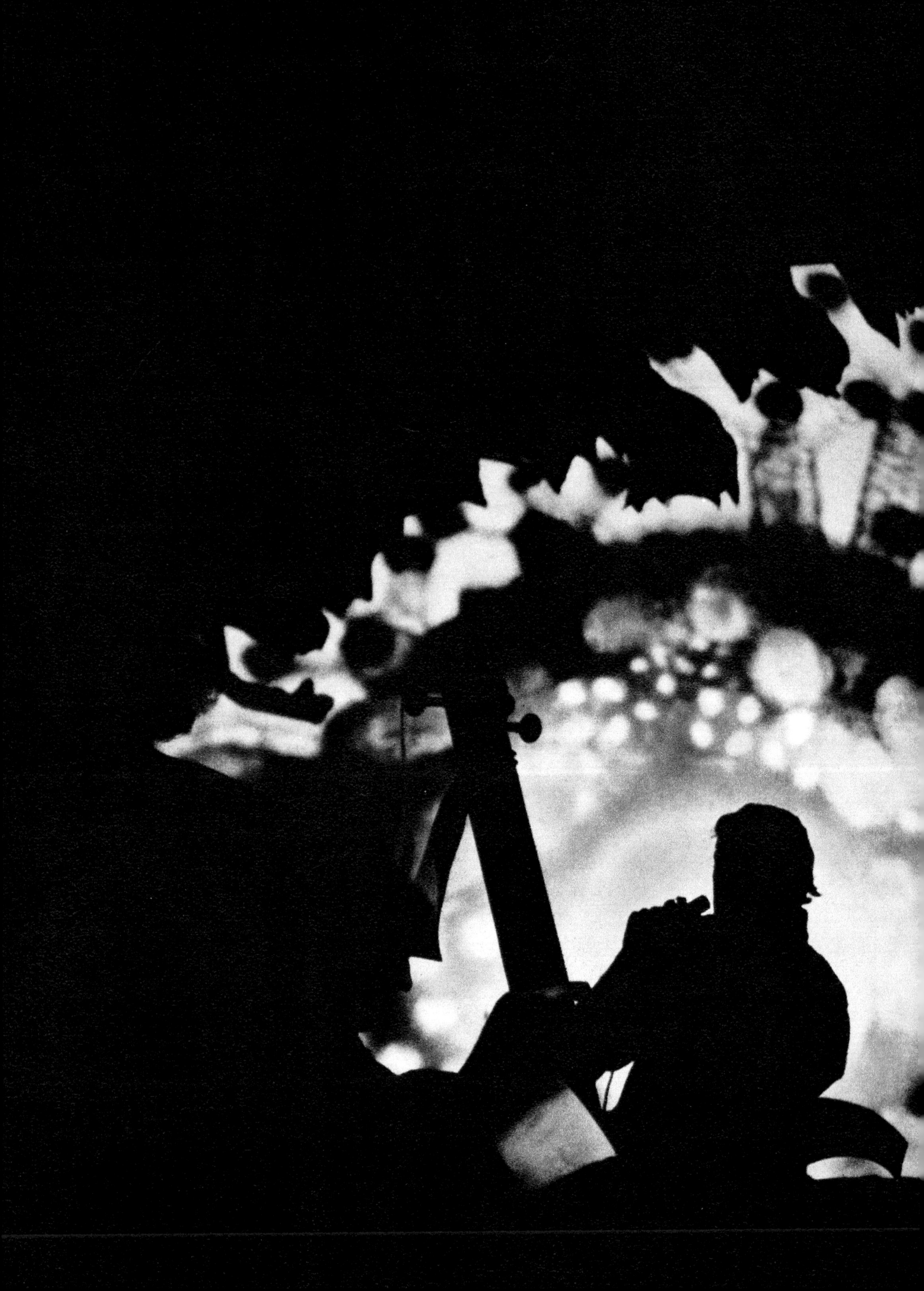

New York City: Fillmore East and Joshua Light Show

Brooklyn: Dynamite discotheque

New York City: Central Park

New York City

Boston, Massachusetts

Chicago, Illinois

New York City: Yippie pig

California: Nudity as protest

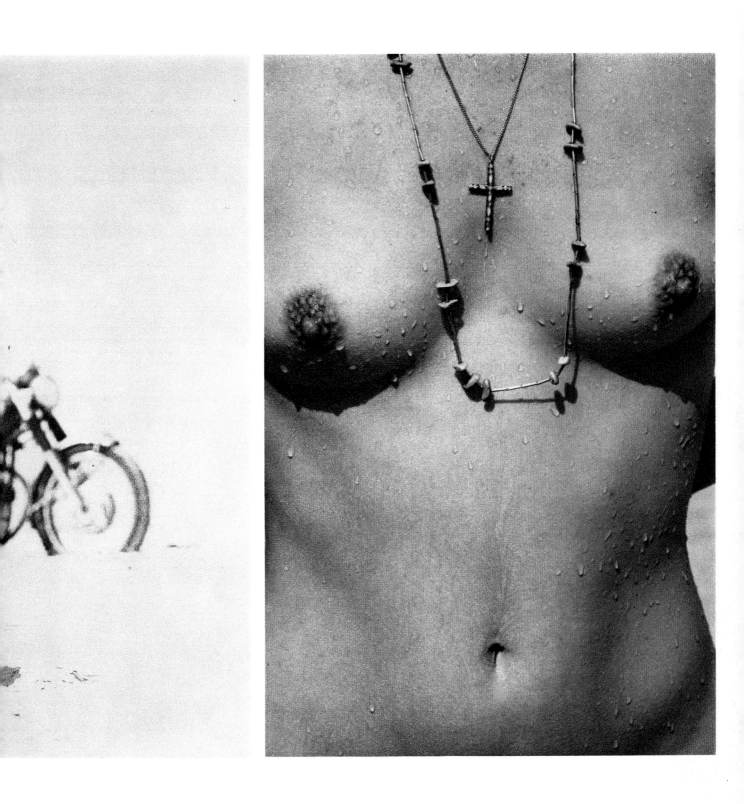

Berkeley, California

An Alternative.
Secluded by the great space of the West,
communities are rising, each with its own style of
architecture and life. Some builders
make adobe shelters, even castles in the mud.
Others dwell in geodesic domes constructed
from the abundant junk America provides.
Pictures by Danny Lyon.

The Political Response

The sound of battle was heard long before delegates gathered for the thirty-fifth Democratic National Convention. Divided by race, by age, and by war, the nation had become more and more jumpy; to use the diagnosis popular among the oversophisticated, we were all "paranoid." Whites feared black rioting. Blacks feared white genocide. Radicals feared repression. Police feared radical revolution. The middle class trembled before flower power. College presidents were toppled by student power. Now, in Chicago, the dissident wing of the Democratic Party was split between the grieving followers of Robert Kennedy, who might have won the nomination, and ebullient converts to Eugene McCarthy, who surely could not.

"There was violence inside the International Amphitheater before the violence broke out in Chicago streets," recalled playwright Arthur Miller, a McCarthy delegate from Connecticut. "One knew from the sight of barbed wire topping the cyclone. fence surrounding the vast parking lot, from the emanations of hostility in the credential-inspecting police that something had to happen." The nervous city, transformed into a bristling fortress, was ready to fight on two fronts: to quell any August uprising in the ghetto and to avoid disruption of the convention by several thousand youths who planned to protest under the banner of the "Mobe"—the National Mobilization Committee to End the War in Vietnam.

Mayor Richard Daley's countermobilization put 12,000 city police on twelve-hour shifts and ringed the barricaded convention hall with a special 2,000-man force. Backing up this small army of constabulary was a small army of soldiers—6,000 men of the Illinois National Guard, plus 6,000 Regular Army troops who had been airlifted to Chicago in full combat gear—rifles, bazookas, and flamethrowers.

For those who believed that the city was over-prepared, the Mayor had an explanation. "This administration has always taken the position that an ounce of prevention is worth a pound of cure," he said. Adding a few more ounces, the Mayor also denied all parade permits within a stone's throw of the Amphitheater and issued orders to strictly enforce regulations against sleeping in lakeside Lincoln Park.

Although the Mobe optimistically estimated a turnout of one hundred thousand protesters (a projection which partly accounts for the size of the garrison), no more than ten thousand showed up, and probably half of these lived in or near Chicago. These were young Democrats who opposed Hubert Humphrey, unaffiliated antiwar students, Yippies, hippies, and radical Students for a Democratic Society. For all of them, the angry as well as the alienated, the convention was sure to be a well-publicized arena of protest. For some, it was planned as a lot more—a test of confrontation politics which would provoke police into brutal reprisal and demonstrate "fascist repression," expose the "bankruptcy" of liberal politics, and radicalize nonradical innocents.

The strategy succeeded beyond all expectation, but its triumph was due less to the provocations of militants than to the blind ferocity of the police response. For while youths did hurl rocks, bottles, sharp-edged bathroom tiles, and even human feces, officers of the law were seized by mass frenzy. The official report by Daniel Walker, a prominent Chicago attorney, to the National Commission on the Causes and Prevention of Violence concluded that the outbreak could "only be called a police riot." Seen on television throughout the world, it was an astonishing display of political theater. "The whole world is watching," the demonstrators yelled at police; it was both a taunt and a boast.

The riots erupted during four consecutive nights. The first broke out after youths had been forced out of Lincoln Park into the streets of the surrounding neighborhood and the Walker report vividly described the chase that followed: "On the part of the police there was enough wild club swinging, enough cries of hatred, enough gratuitous beating to make the conclusion inescapable that individual policemen, and lots of them, committed violent acts far in excess of the requisite force for crowd dispersal or arrest."

The last outbreak took place in the heart of the city, watched by guests high up in the Conrad Hilton Hotel and by crowds lining Michigan Avenue. Police, breaking up a protest march, quite simply ran amok. On Michigan Avenue and in the side streets leading to the Loop, the report said, "police ranged the streets striking anyone they could catch." Policemen on motorcycles charged into groups of people, while those on foot sprayed Mace, swung fists, and cracked heads, leaving demonstrators, newsmen, and passersby lying on the ground. "That violence was made all the more shocking by the fact that it was often inflicted on persons who had broken no law, disobeyed no orders, made no threat," the report observed. "These included peaceful demonstrators, onlookers, and large numbers of residents who were simply passing through, or happened to live in, the areas where confrontations were occurring."

Television's staring, eyewitness view of the street battle spilled into the Amphitheater just as delegates prepared to vote on the nominations for President. Still, the business of the convention proceeded without pause. The anti-Humphrey forces were outraged. "Gestapo tactics," shouted the normally restrained Senator Abraham Ribicoff, while other angry delegates denounced their host, Mayor Daley, and demanded that the convention adjourn to another city. But the protesters never had a chance. The band played loudly, microphones were cut off, while the uproar—as well as the balloting—continued. Finally, almost as an anticlimax, Humphrey was nominated with 1,761 ¾ votes to Eugene McCarthy's 601. Back at his hotel, the party's Presidential choice closed the blinds of his hotel window against the riot below and kissed his wife's image on the television screen.

The campaign that followed "Bloody Chicago" was pallid, as if the country could no longer endure the emotional pitch of the preceding months. Protests over Vietnam were virtually smothered by the Paris peace talks. Law and order became the primary domestic issue, reflecting the electorate's impatience with ghetto and campus outbursts. Exploiting such popular resentment with demagogic skill, Governor George C. Wallace of Alabama emerged as the only candidate with a fervent and dedicated constituency and the first third-party leader since Henry Wallace to demonstrate a national appeal. Richard Nixon's comfortable lead was threatened during the final weeks of the campaign by Democratic gains that averaged two hundred thousand votes a day; the last-minute surge almost made a dull race exciting.

Humphrey was a decent man trapped by his predecessor's policies; he could not repudiate the President without losing organizational support, nor defend him without losing independent and liberal backing. According to reporter Paul O'Neil, Humphrey gloomily told a friend, "I've inherited all his [Johnson's] enemies but none of his friends." Students and intellectuals were angry over the war. Negroes were dissatisfied. The richest middle class in history was in no mood to pay higher taxes to build the Great Society. Humphrey had been ahead of his time in 1948 as a liberal leader for civil rights, union rights, health insurance, and similar advanced causes. In 1968 he seemed behind the times, or at least out of tune with them.

Humphrey's handicaps were a perverse reflection of Richard Nixon's advantages. Nixon had inherited friends in both wings of the party and enemies in neither. The durable and meticulous draftsman of party unity was nominated in an amiably brisk thirty-three-minute first ballot. Not even the deaths of three Negroes during a riot in the Miami ghetto distracted the convention. The G.O.P. platform, rebuilt over the rubble left by the Goldwater campaign four years earlier, was a masterpiece of generalities that appealed to both liberals and conservatives. If the candidate did not say how he could end the war, it was enough that he promised peace. ("You will not be fighting another Vietnam.") If he did not explain how he would restore "law and order," it was enough that he condemned rioting. ("The first civil right is the right to be free from civil violence.") If he did not disclose plans to halt the rising cost of living, it was enough that he pronounced the virtues of a sound economy. ("Prosperity without war and progress without inflation.") To voters grown weary of Vietnam, worried by black and white militants, and wary of inflation, such rhetoric was comforting, but Nixon's efficient, evasive campaign, like Humphrey's desperate one, touched off little genuine enthusiasm.

Perhaps because George Wallace offered quick and easy solutions, braced by sneering wit and wisecracks, he was a more exciting campaigner than either Nixon or Humphrey, and won over to his side millions of largely lower-middle-class followers. Playing on their resentments, he laughed off "pointy-headed college professors who can't even park a bicycle straight." Negro rioters should be shot: "Bam! Bam! Bam! Right in the head." Student protesters who blocked his car would be promptly run over. He was the voice of the politically voiceless—the clerks and policemen, manual workers and small businessmen who filled his collection buckets with dollar bills. Like them, he was a have-not glowering at the haves. "This is the first time in your history so many big politicos been worried about us," Wallace said, defiantly. "They say we going to hurt 'em, and I'll tell you something: I *want* to hurt 'em, 'cause they've hurt us long enough and I'm tired of it."

On Election Day, Wallace polled about thirteen per cent of the vote, considerably less than predicted, due to a large last-minute swing by blue-collar union workers back to their usual Democratic habits. Reflecting general dissatisfaction with the campaign and the major candidates, only sixty per cent of the eligible voters—the smallest percentage in twelve years—went to the polls. Some fifteen million registered voters did not bother to vote. For the first time in one hundred and twenty years, a first-term President and a Congress were elected from different parties. Though Humphrey lost by only half a million votes, Nixon, with 43.4 per cent of the total, emerged a minority President with the smallest share of the total since Woodrow Wilson in 1912. So, while the nation edged over to the right, it did not decisively reject the old liberalism. Republicans did well among white, middle-class, middle-age voters who live in small towns, suburbs, and on farms. Democrats won majorities in cities and ghettoes, among religious and ethnic minorities and young people. Richard Nixon won the votes of those for whom the American Dream may still have meaning, but he had yet to win the allegiance of many for whom the dream has little reality.

Republicans in Miami.

Democrats in Chicago.

Mayor Richard Daley

Chicago: Grant Park

Chicago: Grant Park

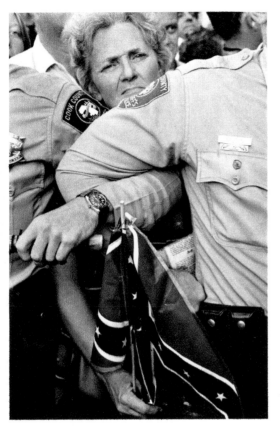

Chicago: Wallace enthusiasts

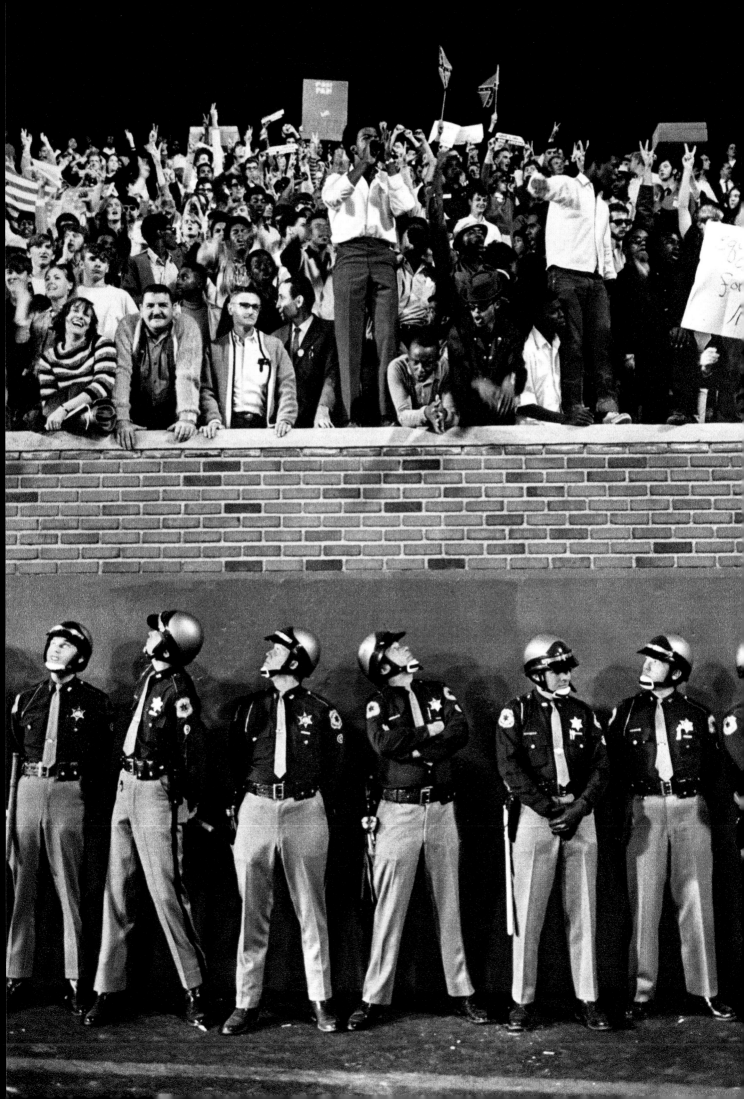

Fleet, Michigan

Mr. and Mrs. Hubert Humphrey on campaign plane

The Quality of American Life

Americans live to the tempo of an "insensate dynamism," Lewis Mumford wrote several years ago; since then the pace has quickened and we seem to be feeling it more acutely. A nation born in optimism and growing up with confidence approaches the end of its second century with its belief in progress weakened. The dark clouds no longer appear to have silver linings; our faith in the future is less comforting, yet we have found no faith to replace it. "We itch," one impatient youth explained, "but we don't know where to scratch."

Certainly one reason for our irritability is widespread doubt whether scratching would make much difference, considering the enormity of the problem: If the age we are entering is technocratic, governed by specialized skills beyond the reach and perhaps the understanding of most citizens, how will democracy survive?

The dilemma was raised in a study of the impact of technology on society, directed by a philosopher-economist, Emmanuel G. Mesthene. "The question is how to take advantage of the knowledge necessary to run a big complex society without giving up the values of participation," he wrote. "The answer we're looking for is a third way. We haven't found it yet." In the meantime, knowledge is increasingly concentrated in huge private corporations and universities. These are remote from the individual (even as they shape his life) and their powers rival those of the government itself. The web of ever-larger organizations, more intricate systems, and more ingenious experts is a continuing marvel of technological achievement, but the strain of maintaining it is enormous and in many respects unrewarding for society. Instant mass communication has created an instant mass culture whose banalities need no itemizing. Clogged jetports have added another dimension to the old complaint, "Hurry up and wait." Automated factories effortlessly deluge the market with attractive products which are then sold with great effort and added expense to consumers who had not previously realized their deprivation. From the corner supermarket to the distant "military-industrial complex," people are manipulated; the feeling that they are powerless is a basic cause of their unrest. The result is disorder in social institutions, isolation in social relations, dissatisfaction with personal lives and national goals.

Not everyone is unhappy, of course, and the country is divided between those who are impatient for reform and those who are impatient with reformers. Speaking with poetic optimism, Kenneth Rexroth has said that "Just because the machine is so vast, so complex, it is far more sensitive than ever before. Individual action does tell. Give a tiny poke at one of the insignificant gears down in its bowels and slowly it begins to shudder all over and suddenly belches out hot rivers." As for the forces of government, they are both ever-present and distant. Two essential political resources—the flexibility of the system and the pragmatism of the response—are in short supply. As Horace Busby, a former White House assistant, declared in a speech to the nation's city managers: "This new American life is strangely hard. Affluence is a vast irrelevancy. As a people we are overworked, overburdened...and on many things, overly anxious....Increasingly, ours is a society slipping out of phase. In sector after sector—from delivery of medical services to the delivery of the mail—we are barely able to do what we are doing, with no assurance how long we can continue."

The same lack of certainty applies to the future of the physical environment, a meeting of crises which is no mere coincidence. A nation, like a man, requires a sound mind in a sound body, and the symptoms of America's internal fever are the country's polluted waters, scarred landscape, poisoned air. The central city is decaying. The shapeless agglomerates of suburbia spread—growing seven times as fast as the inner city. The population growth, despite a current dip in the birth rate, is expected to be booming soon again. Meanwhile, the economic boom continues almost without interruption, with much of the people's wealth spent on luxuries undreamed of in other countries. America's spending on cigarettes and other tobacco products is twice as much as Britain spends on its entire National Health Service; we lavish more on recreation than the combined gross national product of Venezuela, Iran, the Philippines, and Israel. And we blow more each year on the services offered by organized crime—primarily for illegal but socially acceptable gambling on our beloved sports events—than on the Vietnam war.

The Swedish scholar, Gunnar Myrdal, while hopeful that the nation's reservoir of "common explicit morality" will make gradual social progress possible in the long run, nevertheless is gloomy about the short-run reality. "There is," he has said, "an ugly smell rising from the basement of the stately American mansion." The description is not wholly metaphorical. Every day New York City empties two hundred million gallons of raw sewage into the Hudson River. America's homes annually disgorge forty-eight billion cans, twenty-six billion bottles and jars, and sixty-five billion metal and plastic caps—a prodigious squandering that could only flow from prodigal wealth. The average person's yearly production of 1,600 pounds of these solid wastes is growing by four per cent a year—in pace with the rising gross national product. Some seven million vehicles a year are abandoned or pile up in auto junkyards (the figure is expected to dou-

ble or triple in the next thirty years), while ninety million moving vehicles pollute the air, tie up traffic, and are involved in more than half of all disabling accidents. The automobile alone cannot be blamed for the mess. According to Yale conservationist Paul B. Sears, part of the responsibility lies with "a society which regards profit as a supreme value, under the illusion that anything that's technically possible is therefore ethically justified."

Because most waste is neither salvaged nor decays, it must be dumped or burned, adding to the pollution of air and water caused by factories, homes, power plants, and vehicles. The United States Public Health Service estimates that the air we breathe includes more than 140 million tons of pollutants that rise into the atmosphere each year. Water pollution has not only made major rivers, bays, and lakes unfit for man or aquatic beast, but has also aggravated the need for even larger supplies of water for the growing population and its supporting industry and agriculture. Though pollution is worst in metropolitan regions in which seventy per cent of the population now lives, increasing urbanization makes worse pollution a certainty. By 1980, if present trends continue, urban land area will probably rise by fifty per cent; cities and the adjacent "slurbs" will house an additional forty-five million souls; to accommodate them will require paving and building up as much as a million acres of land each year. By the year 2000, when ninety per cent of all Americans are expected to live in cities and when the population is likely to exceed three hundred million, demands for fresh air, clean water, public services, and enough open space for a moment of tranquility will have forced invention of new answers to old questions about the aims and organization of national life. The outcome will determine whether "the stately American mansion" can, or should, survive with its present room arrangement: part bazaar, part discotheque, part slum, and part rumpus room—with a two-car heated garage.

It will also decide whether the American Dream is still worth dreaming, and whether the values of agrarian society should be discarded as obsolete. Rugged individualism is no longer needed to battle the elements; pioneers may have been at the mercy of nature, but man has learned to regulate his environment. The western frontier created a rural America of new opportunities, but with farm jobs disappearing at the rate of three hundred thousand a year the new frontier lies in the cities. Even "liberty for all" now seems an insufficient goal when compared to the demand for equality for all. Yet despite the cultural and economical upheavals that have transformed the United States, elements of the original dream retain a remarkable grip on our consciousness. The farmer is still the heroic archetype, just as the city remains the symbol of venery. Recipients of charity are considered somehow disreputable, as though the unskilled and poorly educated can still hire out their strength. To be rich is to be good, as though touched by grace. We still preserve those Jeffersonian values that are profoundly suspicious of government planning, while ignoring the Jefferson who also urged that "Communities must be planned with an eye to the effect made upon the human spirit by being continuously surrounded with a maximum of beauty."

But if the Dream is sometimes distorted and in some ways outmoded, it has also nourished enviable ideals. Mass education, marred by the deficiencies of mass production, has created the largest and best-trained academic elite ever gathered in one nation. Faith in youth, while undergoing severe tests at the moment, has produced a generation of astonish-ingly self-confident, critical (even overconfident and tyrannically critical) young people, who just might manage to make some improvements before they retreat into early middle age at thirty. Free political discourse—impassioned or cool, some of it ugly—has survived assassination, riot, and anger. As the novelist, Harvey Swados, wrote on his return home after a long stay abroad: "After all the suffering and tragedy this country has inflicted upon others, from its own minorities to Latin America to Southeast Asia, it is still the mecca for countless ordinary people throughout the world, students, workers, intellectuals who would do virtually anything to come here. They dream of America…not just because the Alger myth still lives but because …there adheres to the very name of this country a special quality, a specially precious freedom…." Finally, that historic worship of technology which drove Americans to span a continent and climb toward the moon has also led to our current predicament: whether the widely-acclaimed revolution in knowledge can be made to serve not only man's machines, but his spirit as well.

We can now "invent the future," it has been said, or obliterate it. While technology rushes on, our politics, economics, social structure—even our psychology—vainly strain to keep up. It is a time of jolting change, of endings and beginnings.

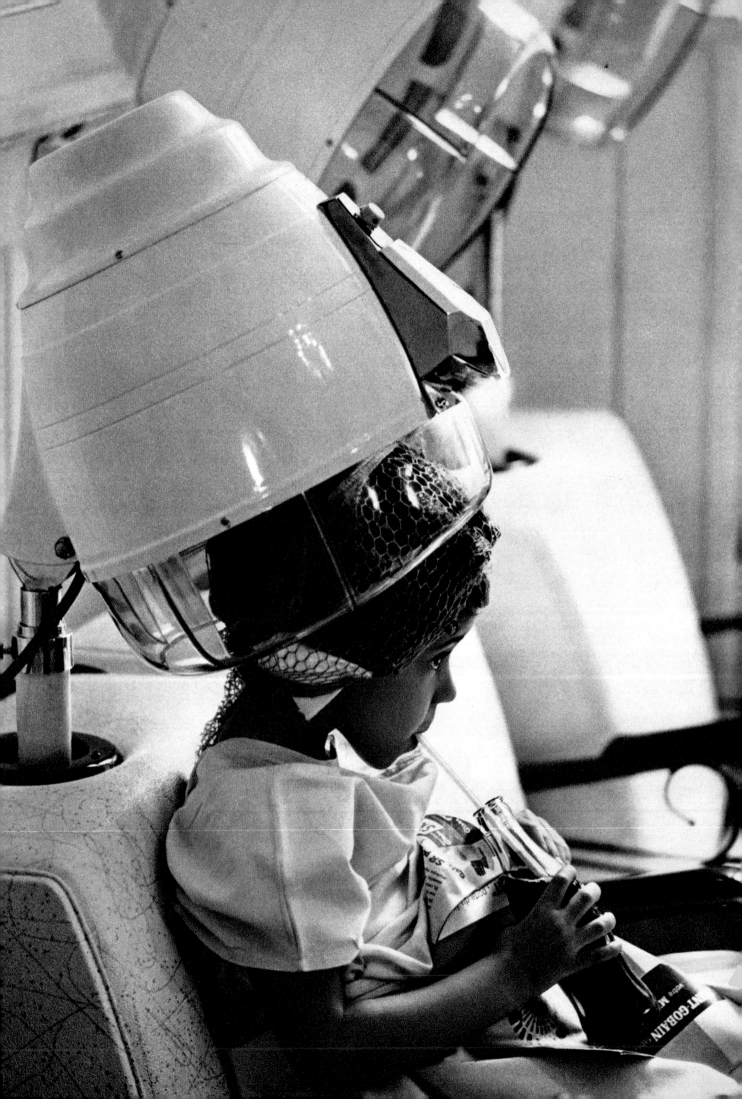

INVENTORY 1983

Photographers' Credits:

FALL 76

INVENTORY 74

10-11 — Charles Harbutt
12-13 — Burk Uzzle
14 — Eve Arnold
15 — Burk Uzzle
16 — Mary Ellen Mark
17 — Charles Harbutt
18 — Charles Harbutt
19 — Burk Uzzle
20 — Top: Elliott Erwitt
    Bottom: Charles Harbutt
21 — Top: Charles Harbutt
    Bottom: Burk Uzzle
22 — Constantine Manos
23 — Charles Harbutt
24 — Dennis Stock
25 — Charles Harbutt
26-27 — Charles Harbutt
30 — Elliott Erwitt
31 — Top: Burk Uzzle
    Bottom: Charles Harbutt
32-33 — Burk Uzzle
34 — Burk Uzzle
35 — Charles Harbutt
36-37 — Top: Charles Harbutt
    Bottom: Burk Uzzle
44-49 — Charles Harbutt
50-55 — Constantine Manos
56 — Charles Harbutt
57 — Burk Uzzle
58-62 — Charles Harbutt

63 — Donald McCullin
69 — Bruce Davidson
70 — Hiroji Kubota
71 — Burk Uzzle
72 — Top: Bruce Davidson
72-73 — Bottom: Danny Lyon
73 — Bruce Davidson
74 — Bruce Davidson
75 — Danny Lyon
76 — Burt Glinn
77 — Left: Burk Uzzle
    Right: Burt Glinn
78 — Burk Uzzle
79 — Roger Malloch
85-93 — Philip Jones Griffiths
94-97 — Donald McCullin
98-101 — Constantine Manos
102-103 — Charles Harbutt
104-105 — Mary Ellen Mark
106-111 — Charles Harbutt
112 — Burt Glinn
113 — Cornell Capa
114-115 — Burt Glinn
116-117 — Cornell Capa
122-123 — Charles Harbutt
124 — Burk Uzzle
125 — Roger Malloch
126-127 — Charles Harbutt
130 — Wayne Miller
131 — Burt Glinn
132 — Left: Constantine Manos
    Right: Charles Harbutt
133 — Left: Roger Malloch
    Right: Charles Harbutt
134 — Paul Ryan
135 — Dennis Stock
136 — Charles Harbutt

137 — Wayne Miller
138-141 — Danny Lyon
145-150 — Elliott Erwitt
151 — Hiroji Kubota
152 — Charles Harbutt
153 — Burt Glinn
154 — Roger Malloch
155 — Top: Mary Ellen Mark
    Bottom: Rick Winsor
156-157 — Charles Harbutt
158-159 — Roger Malloch
160 — Roger Malloch
161 — Mary Ellen Mark
162 — Roger Malloch
163 — Charles Harbutt
164-165 — Roger Malloch
166 — Hiroji Kubota
167 — Bruce Davidson
168-169 — Cornell Capa
170-172 — Elliott Erwitt
173 — Constantine Manos
177 — Elliott Erwitt
178 — Top: Burk Uzzle
    Bottom: Charles Harbutt
179 — Burk Uzzle
180-181 — Charles Harbutt
182-183 — Cornell Capa
184 — Burk Uzzle
185 — Charles Harbutt
186-191 — Bruce Davidson